Burns and Lambert

Origin of the Holy Scriptures

Their progress, transmission, corruptions, and true character

Burns and Lambert

Origin of the Holy Scriptures
Their progress, transmission, corruptions, and true character

ISBN/EAN: 9783741197710

Manufactured in Europe, USA, Canada, Australia, Japa

Cover: Foto ©Lupo / pixelio.de

Manufactured and distributed by brebook publishing software (www.brebook.com)

Burns and Lambert

Origin of the Holy Scriptures

ORIGIN

OF THE

HOLY SCRIPTURES;

THEIR

PROGRESS, TRANSMISSION,

CORRUPTIONS,

AND

TRUE CHARACTER.

Second Edition.

"Thinkest thou that thou understandest what thou readest? Who said: And how can I, unless some man show me?—ACTS viii. 30, 31.

LONDON:
BURNS & LAMBERT, 17 PORTMAN STREET.
DUBLIN, LONDON, & DERBY: RICHARDSON & SON.
EDINBURGH: J. MILLER.
1864.

EDINBURGH: PRINTED BY J. MILLER, 27 COCKBURN STREET.

Preface.

In presenting the present little volume to a Protestant Bible-reading Public, and to his beloved fellow-Catholics, the author hopes to be pardoned for his presumption in entering upon so vast a question as that of Bible controversy; but the absence of any short and simple account—for the instruction of ordinary readers like himself—of the origin, preservation, transmission and corruptions of the Holy Scriptures, induced him to commit to writing in the present connected form, the information he had gathered on these points; to discuss at the same time, and in a brief manner, the nature of the Bible, and to show to the Protestant reader the fallacy, of elevating it into the sole rule of faith of the Christian.

In the researches which the writer made, first for his own instruction, and which, he hopes, will now be welcome to the general inquirer into the Bible question, he had recourse to the following eminent Catholic works, from most of which, as to historical facts, datas, corruptions, &c., he made copious extracts; they are:—

Alban Butler's Lives of the Saints,
The "Dublin Review,"
Ward's Errata,

Dr Wiseman's Lectures,
Spalding's Refutation of D'Aubigny's History of the Swiss Reformation, and
Bossuet's Variations.

Besides these works, the writer has drawn abundantly from those of learned Protestants, which, however, it is not necessary here to enumerate, as they are named wherever their labours have been made use of in this compilation, whilst the former, for the sake of simplicity, are mostly not specially referred to.

In perusing this little treatise, the reader will be good enough to observe, that all sentences within parenthesis, are remarks of the author, and do not belong to the quotations from the Bible between which they are interspersed.

THE AUTHOR.

To the Protestant Reader.

THE present work will speak for itself as to its design; but owing to some expressions therein made use of respecting heretics and wilful perverters of the gospel, it would be wrong to create in you the impression, that it has been written with any uncharitable feeling towards non-Catholics, or with the least intention of wounding in any way the sincere, though Protestant Christian, whilst the very opposite motives and sentiments actuated the author in this compilation; it therefore becomes necessary, first of all, to explain, what is meant by the word "heretic," as applied by the Catholic Church, and also, what means, that "there is no salvation except in her."

That there have been heretics, that there are still, and always will be such to the end of the world, the Holy Scriptures abundantly testify; the apostle anathematized them as the *destroyers of souls*, as ravening wolves, and they are, unfortunately, no fiction.

A heretic, then, is such a one, who, knowing the Catholic Church to be the Church of Christ, falls off from the same, and impugns her faith and doctrines; or a person who, without being a member of the true Church, knows her doctrines to be divine and true, yet favours error, and opposes her teaching. Those, who from ignorance fall off from the Church, as well as those who, from invincible ignorance, that is, from an ignorance which is not their own fault, are opposed to her, and remain separated from her communion, are not classed among the company of heretics. Consequently, any remarks made, which seemingly might be hurtful to a sincere Protestant inquirer, are solely applicable to, and meant for, *wilful defamers* of the doctrines and practices of the Catholic Church, and for *intentional preverters* of the pure word of God, whether written or unwritten; and that these deserve the severest censure, no one will or can deny, as every candid mind must agree, that, though the doctrines of any community may honestly be questioned, sifted, and assailed even, yet, that they must not be *defamed*, that they must not be represented as different from what *they are*, different from what the respective community teaches them to be, and to mean.

"That there is no salvation except in the Catholic Church," simply means: "that the Catholic Church *alone* is able to save mankind."

Christ came and founded but *one* religion, but *one Church*, to save man; consequently, there is but *one religion*, but *one Church*, which actually can save us, and *no other*. This alone saving religion is the faith of Catholics; the only saving Church, the Catholic Church; therefore: whoever wishes to be saved, *must embrace* her faith, *must join* her communion. By this it is not meant to say, that *all Catholics will be saved*, nor, that all Protestants, or all other dissenters from the Catholic Church, will be lost. This only is *certain:* that if a Catholic earnestly desire to be saved, *his religion, the religion of his Church, can and will save him*, if he practice it faithfully; but a Protestant *cannot be saved by means of his church, or sect, or religion;* if through the mercy of God he be saved,—and it is to be hoped that thousands will—it is not *in virtue of his religion*, or of his clinging to the community he belongs to, but in virtue of something else which we do not know, in virtue, for instance, of his invincible ignorance of the Catholic faith, of an ignorance not arising from culpable neglect, indifference, &c. Christ gave us but *one* saving religion, *not two*, but *one* saving Church, *not two;* therefore: there is but *one religion*, but *one Church* that can save man, and not another, or others, besides.

That you, dear Protestant reader, may soon find this one saving faith and embrace it, soon find this *alone* saving Church and join it, has been the chief and fondly cherished object of

THE AUTHOR.

Contents.

	Pages.
The nature of religion; God's method of communicating it to man, and its propagation before the coming of Christ	1— 5
Verbal propagation of the Gospel, the faith in our Saviour Jesus Christ	5— 8
Propagation of the Gospel, or good tidings, by a *written* rule of faith, by the Bible	8—10
The sacred volume is not, *in any case*, an exclusive rule of faith	11—15
Review of the preceding propositions	15—
Why were the Gospels and Epistles of the New Testament ever written?	16—17
The History of each of the Gospels and Epistles in particular	17—20
1. The Gospel of St. Matthew	17—20
2. ,, ,, Mark	20—21
3. ,, ,, Luke	21—22
4. ,, ,, John	22—23
5. The Acts of the Apostles	23—25
6. The Epistle of St. Paul to the Romans	25—26
7. ,, I. ,, ,, Corinthians	26—28
8. ,, II. ,, ,, ,,	28—
9. ,, ,, Galatians	29—30
10. The Epistle of St. Paul to the Ephesians	30—33
11. ,, ,, Philippians	33—35
12. ,, ,, Colossians	35—37
13. ,, I. ,, ,, Thessalonians	37—38
14. ,, II. ,, ,, ,,	38—39
15. ,, I. ,, ,, Timothy	39—41
16. ,, II. ,, ,, ,,	41—42
17. ,, ,, Titus	42—43

CONTENTS.

	Pages.
18. The Epistle of St. Paul to Philemon	43—
19. ,, ,, Hebrews	43—44
20. The Catholic Epistle of St. James	44—46
21. The I. Epistle of St. Peter	46—48
22. The II. Epistle of St Peter	48—49
23. The I. Epistle of St. John	49—50
24. The II. Epistle of St. John	50—51
25. The III. Epistle of St. John	51—
26. The Catholic Epistle of St. Jude	51—52
27. The Apocalypse of St. John	52—55
A few words on the chief aim of the Gospels and Epistles	55—58
Proof from reason that the Bible *cannot* be a rule of faith	58—64
How are we sure, whether the Bible is actually the word of God?	64—70
Progress of this sacred book, from the Apostles' down to our present time	70—75
The New Testament	75—108
The Canon of the Holy Scriptures	108—118
Preservation of the purity and correctness of the text of the sacred writings	119—131
The true sense of the sacred writings	132—155
When did the Bible supersede the authority of the Catholic Church?	156—158
Recapitulation	158—160
Conclusion. The true character of the written word of God	161—

Origin of the Holy Scriptures, &c.

THE NATURE OF RELIGION; GOD'S METHOD OF COMMUNICATING IT TO MAN, AND ITS PROPAGATION BEFORE THE COMING OF CHRIST.

RELIGION is "re-union to, or reconciliation with, God;" and man, being created by, and dependent upon, God his Creator, it must necessarily come from Him.

When Adam and Eve offended the love of God, it was God who prescribed to them the means of reconciliation; it was He who imparted to them religion, who revealed it to them. If then religion, the means of re-uniting ourselves to God after we have fallen away from Him, has come, and must come, from Him, in order to be *divine* and *true:* it follows, that *divine* and *true* religion cannot emanate from reason, cannot come from man, because reason itself is a gift of God to man, to the created being. *True* religion, therefore, if it does not, *cannot*, emanate from reason, from man: it must come from God Himself, must be revealed, or imparted, to man by God his Creator. In the same manner, then, as man receives reason, intellect, and every other faculty of soul and body as a gift of God, so *he receives, as a gift of love, as a mark of grace,* His divine religion, by which alone he can obtain pardon; and his reason *submits* to this divine religion because it comes from God, from his Creator, from the Creator of his reasoning faculty.

True religion, then, is not a creation, a production, an invention, or a discovery of reason, nor of any other faculty of the soul, and therefore neither subject to *any attribute* of man, nor capable of being ruled or expounded, much less altered by *any human being;* for, God alone, from whom it comes, can make, rule, and expound it. But *true* religion is the *light* of reason, by which reason is to walk, and by which reasoning man is to seek and find God; it is not a light to be experimented upon by piety and learning, much less by conceited ignorance, wickedness and pride; but it is to *bring reason back to God*, when men, according to St Paul (Ephes. iv. 18), "having their *understanding darkened, are alienated* from the life of God through the ignorance that is in them, because of the blindness of their hearts."

God loved us too much to allow his repenting children, in their anxious desire to return, after they had left Him and lost themselves amid the labyrinths, the mole-holes of vice and error, to experimentalize, or to grope about in uncertainty and darkness. No! He sets before them, as their guide, a blazing flame, a divine light, that they may be sure to find again their former home, and their fond, expectant Father. Reason can create, can invent, *no light* for the darkened understanding; like the sapient owl, it can look into darkness, but cannot dispel it, cannot disperse the clouds by which it is enveloped; it must therefore be subject to this heavenly light, to *true religion*, the same as man is subject to the light of day, and not the light to him. As the glorious sun sends forth his rays of light to the material body, so does God, by *manifest revelation*, or by *manifestly and specially appointed messengers*, send the divine rays of true religion to the spiritual soul, to *enlighten* the faculty of reason.

Thus, God imparts, or teaches; the soul receives, or *learns*. In this manner Adam and Eve, after their fall, *learn* from God's merciful *direct revelation;* in this manner He *endowed* their reason with His divine religion, and thus lit up the darkness in which it was *helplessly* dwelling; He fixed, He prescribed the Creator to the creature, as the father to the child, the master to the servant, the sovereign to the subject—those conditions, those acts of faith and homage, such as sacrifice, the belief in a future Redeemer, &c., the practice of which He would accept as a means of reconciliation. By *word of mouth* our first parents taught this revealed religion, these heavenly dispensations, to their children; these children *learnt it from them*, and in turn taught it to their descendants, thus creating, through their posterity, and particularly through the visible line of patriarchs, the *chain of tradition.*

When passions had begun to darken men's understanding (St. Paul, Ephe. iv. 18), to shut out and eclipse the light of revelation; when human reason would exalt itself above God, manifest in His religion; when the taper of mortality would outshine the sun of eternity: prophets appeared from time to time, with miracles, the *testimony of heaven*, in their favour, confirming, re-establishing, and further developing the religion once revealed to our first parents; they *taught* the people, and the people *learned.* When the revelations of God, propagated for 2000 years *by tradition*, from generation to generation, had been written down by Moses and succeeding prophets, there remained still, besides this written word of God, the successors of himself and Aaron, the priesthood, by God appointed —though not guided by the Holy Ghost, as were the apostles and their successors—to explain the *duties of the law* and *to teach;* the written code (which did not embrace the whole tradition) for 2000 years, until the coming of Christ, did *not diminish, much less abrogate or supersede*, the authority of the Jewish priesthood, *though not infallible* in their teaching; and thus we find, down to the time of our Saviour, the Sanhedrim, the ecclesiastical council of the Jews, to be the guide, the *teacher* of the people, and their authority to be the *only evidence* and *sole interpreter* of the sacred writings, of their written code of law. The high priest, by command of God, still offered sacrifice; his authority was *undiminished* when the High Priest after the order of Melchisedech appeared; and in the same manner will the authority of Christ's Vicar on earth remain undiminished, until He will again appear in the clouds at the last day.

When our Saviour came; when in Him, who superseded the authority of the old Church, the prophecies of the old covenant were being fulfilled: the rule of faith, the written law, of which the Jewish priesthood boasted, and in which, as Christ told them, they THOUGHT to have life eternal, naturally failed them; —for, *no prophecy of Scripture is of private interpretation* (2 St. Peter i. 20); they neither had the promise of the Holy Ghost to guide them into all truth to the consummation of the world, nor the grace of God in their souls, their "understanding being darkened by the blindness of their hearts;" and thus, they no more found in the Old Testament the testimony of Christ, who in the glory of His spotless life and of His miracles was then present before them, than Protestants find in the New Testament the testimony of the Catholic Church, the standing miracle of our Redeemer these 1800 years. As Christ referred the Jews to their own pretended rule of faith, the written law, for a testimony of Himself: so does the Church of Christ refer Protestants to their own self-made rule of faith for the confirmation of her divine authority.

If then hitherto, *besides tradition*, the Old Testament had served as a statute book, we will even say as a rule of faith, *to the priesthood:* our Saviour came to supersede both, and to concentrate all authority within Himself, within the *Word Incarnate*, from whom this authority had also emanated. As the Son of God, the Redeemer promised to Adam and Eve and their posterity, He perfected, He completed the revelation of His Father; He, instead of the scribes, became the expounder—when the law in Him was fulfilled—of the law, and the founder of the new and more glorious and consoling covenant with God.

This new covenant, this perfected religion, these final conditions, these final means of reconciliation, Christ Himself revealed by *verbal teaching*. This new covenant was to be *taught* to be *preached*, to every nation until the end of the world, by ambassadors whom He Himself would appoint; by a ministry, which He Himself would consolidate: just as the old covenant had been revealed by His Father, transmitted and developed by the patriarchs and prophets, and *taught* by a divinely appointed, though not infallible ministry, until His own coming.

That the *perfected* revelation of our Saviour, the light, that divine and true religion, the gospel, which was to gladden every one that cometh into this world, was to be the safeguard, the polar star of our reason, and not its football; was *intended* and *commanded* by Him to be imparted to man, to be propagated all over the globe, *by authority, by authoritative, unquestionable, verbal teaching;* that it was to be *learned* by *hearing only:* we see *positively, without any equivocation* or *condition,* set forth by St. Paul.

Respecting this

VERBAL PROPAGATION OF THE GOSPEL, THE FAITH IN OUR SAVIOUR JESUS CHRIST,

the apostle says:—"How then shall they call on Him (Jesus) in whom they have not believed? or how shall they believe Him of whom they have not HEARD? And how shall they HEAR without a *preacher?* And how shall they *preach* unless they *be sent? Faith then cometh by* HEARING: (where did the Reformers HEAR the faith they taught and preached, and who sent them?(and *hearing* by the word of God. (Rom. x. 14, 15, 17.)

St. Paul here enters unmistakingly into the ground work, the *main* rule of faith, which our Saviour both *intended* and *commanded;* and that verbal teaching is the *true rule* of faith, we learn:—

1st. *From Christ's own example;* for He only taught by word of mouth, and never committed anything to writing.

2dly. We do learn this in the most positive manner from the sacred writings themselves, viz. :—"And Jesus coming *spoke* to them, saying: All power is given to Me in heaven and on earth. Going therefore *teach ye all nations:* baptizing them in the name of the Father, and of the Son, and of the Holy Ghost, *teaching* them to *observe all things* whatsoever I have commanded you: (nothing had been written down yet), and *behold I am with you all days*, even to the consummation of the world." (St. Mark xxviii. 18, 19, 20.)

Our Saviour gave *no writing* to the apostles for *their guidance*, but said to them: "the Paraclete, the Holy Ghost, whom the Father will send in My name, HE *will teach you all things*, (things that were not written), and bring all things to your mind, whatsoever I shall have *said* to you." (St. John xx. 21.)

Following up this *charge of teaching*, and the *obligation of hearing*, Christ says, on another occasion, to His apostles: "He that *heareth you* (the apostles and their lawfully appointed successors) *heareth Me:* and he that *despiseth you despiseth Me*, and he that despiseth Me, despiseth Him that sent Me." (St. Luke x. 16.) "And if he will not hear the Church,* let him be to thee as the heathen and the publican." (St. Matt. xviii. 17.) St. John, confirming this doctrine of our divine Redeemer, writes in his first epistle (iv. 6):—"He that is not of God, *heareth us not* (namely, the pastors of the same Catholic Church, which was then, is now, and will continue to the end

---

* The *rulers* of course, and not the congregations of that, at the time of the apostles, small *visible* body. which they called catholic, and which since then, like the mustard tree, has grown up to be more visible, extending like it, and still bearing *the name of its infancy.*

of the world). BY THIS (not *hearing those* who have to *rule* the Church of God), we know the spirit of *truth* and the spirit of ERROR."

Hear St. Paul to the same effect; he *commands*, not to obey his written instructions, or to be subject to the Bible, but: "Obey *your prelates* and be subject *to them*." (Hebrews xiii. 17.) Pay attention to what he further enjoins:—"Now I *beseech* you, brethren, to mark them who make dissensions (the Catholic Church made none), and offences contrary to the doctrine (not which he has written or was writing to them, but which you have *learnt* (by hearing), and to avoid them." (Rom. xvi. 17.) "Only there are SOME (not the church) that trouble you, and would pervert the gospel (which the apostles and *their disciples* were *preaching* at the time) of Christ. But though we, or an angel from heaven, preach a gospel to you, *besides that* which we have *preached* to you, let him be anathema. If any one preach to you a gospel, *besides* that which you *have* received (by hearing), let him be anathema." St. Paul wrote this to the Galatians, (i. 7, 8, 9,) when he had hardly commenced his epistle to them; which shows clearly, that they had received the gospel *by hearing*, before he put his pen to parchment. The same apostle continues moreover:— "Therefore, brethren, stand fast; and hold *the traditions* (he calls his epistle a tradition) which you have learned, *whether by our word*, or by our epistle." (2 Thess. ii. 14.) And St. Paul did right to call his epistle a tradition, for, whatever he knew himself, he only knew from tradition; and all his epistles are nothing but *written traditions*, which he enjoins his flock to hold fast. To St. Timothy he writes:— "Keep that which is *committed to thy trust* (not in writing, but something committed to him by word of mouth before the apostle wrote), avoiding the *profane novelties of words*, and *opposition of knowledge, falsely so called*." (1 Tim. vi. 20.) "And the things which thou hast *heard* of me by *many witnesses*, the same *commend* (not to writing, but) to *faithful men*, who shall be fit to *teach* others also." (2 Tim. ii. 2.) "These things *command and teach*." (1 Tim. iv. 2.) To Titus, whom St. Paul had ordained pastor, he writes:— " These things *speak*, (as pastor), and exhort and rebuke with all *authority*." (Titus ii. 15.) And in the Acts (xv. 41), we read that St. Paul "went through Syria and Silicia, confirming the churches, *commanding* them (not to scrutinise or to reject, but) to keep the precepts (which they had from *hearing*, and of which *nothing is said in the Bible*) of the apostles and *ancients*."

Undeniable as it must appear to every honest mind, that the one true religion of our Saviour, according to the preceding texts, was to be propagated by *preaching* and *teaching*, and that it was to be learned from *hearing;* yet we hear those ask, who would fain maintain the

PROPAGATION OF THE GOSPEL, OR GOOD TIDINGS, BY A WRITTEN RULE OF FAITH, BY THE BIBLE:

Why does our Saviour command us, to " Search the Scriptures," adding: " for you think in them to have life everlasting; and the same are they that testify of me?" (St. John v. 39.) Why does St. Paul say to Timothy, " That the holy Scriptures are able to make thee wise (instruct thee) unto salvation through faith which is in Christ Jesus? All Scripture is given by inspiration of God, and is profitable for doctrine, for reproof, for correction, for instruction in righteousness." (2 Tim. iii. 15, 16.) And why does the same apostle commend the Bereans, for "daily searching the Scriptures whether these things were so?" (Acts xvii. 11.)

In the first of the above passages, our Saviour refers the Jews to the Scriptures for a testimony of His divine mission, which they denied. The Bible, in their mind, was their salvation, it was with them their highest authority. Now to that very authority our Saviour appeals to prove His own; and to disabuse them at the same time of their *over* estimation of the sacred writings, He says, as it were : " You deny My divine mission ;—very well ; search the Scriptures, your pretended highest, your exclusive authority ; examine your own witness, for YOU THINK (you THINK so) in them to have life everlasting ; and yet, the very same are they that give testimony of Me, of My superior authority." Thus, Christ said to the Jews, " Search the Scriptures ;" not that they were to make it their rule of faith, but in order to confound them by their own standard, by their own weapon. It is the very same thing with the Catholic Church and all those who dissent from her; with the *very same efficacy and truth* can she rebuke and warn all those who disown her divine authority ; with the very words addressed by our Redeemer to the scribes and Pharisees she can and does address all Protestants : " Search the Scriptures, that very book upon which *alone* you rely, and in which alone you THINK, you find life everlasting ; for it is this very book, these very Scriptures, that testify of me almost on every page, that proclaim and confirm my authority." If the Old Testament was the rule of faith of the Jews, the authority of Christ, even of the Jewish priesthood, was superior : in the same manner is the authority of the Church superior to both the Old and the New Testament.

That we cannot rely on the Scriptures for our salvation, that it will not do to THINK we have it therein, is thus not only quite clear, but confirmed even by the second of the above texts :—" The Holy Scriptures are *able (not certain)* to make thee *wise* (to *instruct* thee) unto salvation, THROUGH FAITH WHICH IS IN CHRIST JESUS." This faith in Christ Jesus, THROUGH WHICH the Scriptures are *able* (not *certain*, even *with* this faith) to make Timothy, the pastor, *wise* unto salvation (not to *save* him, but only *able* to make him wise for *to be saved*), must *precede* the reading of the Scripture; and to precede it, this faith must have been learnt from *hearing*, for faith cometh from *hearing*. Timothy possessed *that faith* from *hearing*, for he could not have learnt it from the Old Testament, of which alone our Saviour and St. Paul speak, as the New one did not yet exist. St. Paul, in addressing Timothy *as a pastor* of the Church, confirms the foregoing text, by saying of the (Old) Scriptures:—" That (in the hands of the pastor) they are *profitable* (mind, *profitable* only, not *saving*) for doctrine, for reproof, for correction, for instruction in righteousness." That the office of *preaching* the word, of reproving, rebuking, exhorting, with all long suffering and doctrine, for which the Bible is *profitable*, belongs to the pastors of the Church alone, is proved by the apostle's charging Timothy most solemnly (2 Tim. iv. 1, 2) with these duties, but only in virtue of Timothy's capacity of pastor and preacher of the Church, the laity being totally out of question. To the pastor, to the bishop even, the Scriptures were only to be *profitable* for certain purposes, *for a confirmation of his own authority;* they were not to be his rule of faith, much less the sole standard of the laity. That the Scriptures, however, are able also to make the laity *wise* unto salvation; that they are profitable to be read *through faith*, learned, previously to reading, from a true, but not from a false, teacher, we are assured of by St. Paul himself, who " commended the Bereans for daily searching the Scriptures" (which was the Old Testament), not in order to learn, find out, or make to themselves some faith or other, but to ascertain, to confirm themselves, whether those things were so which they had *learnt before*, or were just learning, through *verbal teaching*.

Thus, these texts, apart from their referring only to the Old Testament, are not even a command, or injunction, to *read* the Bible, much less to make it

THE SACRED VOLUME IS NOT, *in any case*,
AN EXCLUSIVE RULE OF FAITH.

but rather the reverse, as we do not only learn from tradition, but from the *positive* and *unequivocal* texts of the Prince of the Apostles. We read in St. Paul (2 Tim. iii. 16) :—" That all Scripture is given by inspiration of God," as we learn also from 2 St. Peter (i. 21), by whom we are earnestly warned in the preceding verse of the same chapter :—" That no prophecy of Scripture is of *any private interpretation.*" And speaking of the epistles of the Apostle of the Gentiles, St. Peter says, in his second epistle, (iii. 16) : —" As also in all his epistles, speaking in them of these things ; in which are some things *hard to be understood,* which they that are *unlearned* (are you learned, my dear reader ?) and *unstable* (are you stable, not carried about by every wind of doctrine ?) wrest, as they do also the *other Scriptures, unto their own destruction.*"

That, without manifest divine revelation, without the divine teaching either of Christ, or of His apostles and their successors, our reason, our understanding, remains darkened ; that neither reason, nor any other faculty of the soul can penetrate or dispel that darkness ; that, therefore, true religion must come from God, to vivify and enlighten our reason ; that, on this account, also, the Scriptures never were nor could be intended as a rule of faith, without lawfully appointed teachers ; that thus St. Peter justly passes his unqualified condemnation on *any* private interpretation of the written word of God : we learn most clearly from our Saviour and the apostles. St. Luke, namely, tells us, (xxiv. 45) :—" Then He (Christ) *opened their understanding* (by verbal teaching) that they might *understand the Scriptures.*" Thus, even the apostles could not understand the Scriptures without teaching, to which they had to submit. We further read in the Acts (ix. 30, 31), of a disciple of Christ, who himself had *learned from hearing*, that he addresses the Eunuch in these words :—" Thinkest thou that thou understandest what thou readest ?" To which the man of station, and of learning too, right modestly replied :—" And how can I, unless *some man show* (verbally teach) me ?" Address the question of Philip, the deacon, candidly to yourself, my dear reader! Or do you think to be more privileged, to stand higher than the apostles? higher than the Eunuch, who, at *that time*, could both *possess* and *read* the Scriptures?

Again, we find that Christ, after His resurrection, walking with two of His disciples to Emaus, was obliged to *expound*, to explain to them the meaning of the Scriptures : " And beginning at *Moses and all the prophets, He expounded to them* in all the Scriptures the things that were concerning Him." Their reason had not yet been enlightened, though they had been three years with Christ, hearing His instructions, and going through a course of studies, which few, now-a-days, apart even of the Divine Master, can ever find time for; and though they *knew*, they did not, on that account, *understand* the Scriptures; and hence the *necessity* of a divine teacher.

Some Protestant writers, unenlightened by the rays of divine revelation or authoritative teaching, in their consequent darkness of understanding, thickened perhaps by the blind self-sufficiency of their hearts, have fallen into the strange mistake in which others have prejudiciously followed them, of attempting to prove the Bible to be the sole and only standard and source of truth :

First, from the reference made to the Holy Scriptures by our Saviour, as well as by the devil, when the latter tempted Him. By this joint quotation of our Saviour and of the devil from the same book, these men think they have proved the rule. They are right in so far as the devil wished to make the rule; but Christ, confounding him by his own weapons, drove him away by His *divine authority*. Thus, the Church of Christ is not afraid nor backward to wield the arrogated weapon of her enemies, and, like Christ, both able and successful in confounding and overcoming them by the same means. These writers have tried to prove their rule of faith

Secondly: from the various instances in which Christ addresses the chief priests and Pharisees ; as for instance :—" *Have you never read,* out of the mouth of infants," &c. " *Have you never read in the Scriptures,* the stone which the builders rejected," &c., and in St. Matthew, addressing the Sadducees on the resurrection :—" *You err, not knowing* (which is, *understanding*) *the Scriptures,* nor the power of God ;" and Christ's further proving their error by a reference to Scripture :—" *Have you not read* (among other things) that which was spoken by God," &c. ; also, addressing a certain lawyer (St. Luke x. 25, 26) : " What is *written* in the law ? How *readest thou ?*"

Thirdly: Protestants refer again to St. Paul, where according to his custom in the synagogue, " *he reasoned with the Jews out of the Scriptures,* declaring the suffering and resurrection of Christ whom he was *preaching.*" They also refer to Acts xviii. 28, where " Apollo, with much vigour, convinced the Jews openly, showing by *the Scriptures* that Jesus is the Christ."

Now all these texts, and similar ones without exception, on *their* (Protestant's) *own showing,* are just as many condemnations of the Scriptures as a rule of faith. The devil, the chief priests, the scribes, the Pharisees, the Sadducees, the lawyer, the Jews in the synagogue, all had read and knew (as Protestants now read and know) the Scriptures ; and though *the devil* no doubt *understood* them, it is charitably to be supposed,—as was the case with the apostles and disciples of our Saviour, *before he opened their understanding,* that they might *understand* the Scriptures, —that the others *actually did not understand them,* that their *understanding was still darkened,* and that at least they did *not wilfully wrest their rule of faith, the texts of Scripture*, to their own destruction. However, this perversion of their mind, whether wilful or in *culpable* blindness, shows the utter fallacy of the Scriptures as a rule of faith, because by that rule they were led into error, perhaps to destruction, and because by that very rule, by its plausibility, the devil was induced, even to tempt our Saviour. Alas! how many souls has he not tempted and destroyed thereby! It was on account of the Bible *not being understood* by those who had made it their rule, that our Saviour, the direct revelation, the Divine Revealer of it Himself, had to expound it ; that the apostles, enlightened by the teaching of our Saviour and by the descent of the Holy Ghost, had to *explain* the Scriptures, and to *reason upon them for days* with the obstinate Jews ; that the Church of Christ, of the apostles and their successors, having the promised guidance of the Holy Ghost unto the end of the world, has for centuries had, and still has to battle on the same ground with those, who, like the Jews, make the Bible their exclusive rule of faith, and who, like them, thereby are led into error and opposition to our Saviour and His Church. In the hands of divinely instituted authority, the Bible is the word of God ; but in the hands of unenlightened reason, of unauthorized, self-constituted expounders, it is a book of perdition. (2 St. Peter iii. 16.) You, my dear Christian reader, cannot fail to see this; therefore choose your standard ! either under the banner of Christ, of His apostles, of their manifest successors, of the various flocks of nations and tribes and tongues, harmoniously gathered around it, and in religion submitting their reason to the manifestly divine authority of His, the whole world embracing Church, or under the flying and lying colours of the devil, the scribes, the Pharisees, the preachers of new Gospels, the self-willed, self-opinionated private interpreters of the Scriptures, and among his thousand shaded congregation of sectarianism and confusion : choose, for choose you must, but *bear in mind:* "THAT NO PROPHECY OF SCRIPTURE IS OF PRIVATE INTERPRETATION."

REVIEW OF THE PRECEDING PROPOSITIONS.

If now we have seen, that man cannot possess true religion—of which there is but one—from his own reason, but that, to be true, it must *manifestly* have been revealed to him by God, or that it must have been imparted to him by the *verbal teaching* of a divinely commissioned authority, of neither of which any of the Reformers so-called could boast ; if we have seen that man cannot have faith *except from hearing;* that Christ commanded *preaching and verbal teaching,* after having practised it *exclusively* Himself ; that, in consequence, the apostles propagated the faith by *preaching* and *teaching,* only five of them having written any thing at all ; that they commanded their successors to *teach,* and to appoint others, fit and faithful also for the *office of teaching;* that they enjoined the pastors to hold fast, even *the form of sound words,* (2 Tim. 1. 13) ; that Christ has warned us, as He did the Jews, *not* to THINK that in the Bible we have eternal life ; that the Scriptures are only good for us *through faith in Christ,* in which we must read them, and which on that account we must *previously* have learned from *hearing,* and from preachers *lawfully sent;* that the sacred writings are not even an exclusive rule of faith to the individual pastors, but only profitable to them in the exercise of their ministry, in teaching, reproving, correcting ; that the Scriptures cannot be understood without the teaching of lawful authority, and that therefore, also, it is positively prohibited to put upon them *any private interpretation:* the question may be raised.

WHY WERE THE GOSPELS AND EPISTLES OF THE NEW TESTAMENT EVER WRITTEN?

To this is to be answered :
1st. The gospels were written by the evangelists as *short histories* of the life of Christ, but not as rules of faith; they were written, partly at the request of their respective converts; partly to confirm things already preached and taught; and partly to supply omissions in the histories of Christ, already written by one or two of the evangelists. Two of them wrote as actual eyewitnesses of what they related, and two wrote *from tradition.*

2ndly. The Acts of the Apostles were written as a short history of the Christian Church (called Catholic since her foundation), and on the very face of it, not as a rule of faith, nor as a code of laws, nor as an enumeration and exposition of the revelations of Christ.

3rdly. The epistles were mostly accidental writings; for it is evident, that, if their respective holy authors had been present with those to whom they wrote, they would have preferred to *preach* and *verbally to teach,* and the epistles would never have been written. However, all were written, partly, to warn the various flocks against *false teachers;* to enjoin them, not to wrest the Scriptures to their own destruction, but to be subject and obedient to those whom the Holy Ghost had placed over them. That doctrine and discipline were necessarily interspersed in these missives, as well as in the gospels, is quite natural; but the idea of writing a rule of faith never entered into the minds of the sacred penmen. The only rule of faith, the ground-rule, the basis of all others, left to us by the apostles, professed by the mouth, but belied by the acts of the Established Church, is the Apostle's Creed, of which the Bible does not even breathe a word. In this creed the sincere reader finds, in a very short sentence, the infallible guide to heaven, the

special rule the apostles ever laid down, and this is:—
"I believe in the Holy *Catholic* Church." Believe
her, then, and you will at once belong, in name
and deed, to that very Church which the apostles
founded.

4thly. The Apocalypse, though St. John was told to
write it, is nevertheless no rule of faith, because it is
literally a prophecy, and a mystery, and as such,
above all private interpretation.

Thus we have seen, in general, why the various
books of the New Testament, independent and
separate from each other, were written; this will,
however, appear more clearly on treating of

THE HISTORY OF EACH OF THE GOSPELS AND
EPISTLES IN PARTICULAR.

Commencing in the order of the New Testament,
we have:

1.—THE GOSPEL OF ST. MATTHEW.

St. Matthew, one of the twelve apostles, who from
being a publican, that is, a tax-gatherer, was called
by our Saviour to the apostleship; in that profession
his name was Levi. (St. Luke v. 27, and St. Mark
ii. 14.) He was the first of the evangelists that wrote
the gospel, about six years after our Lord's ascension,
(why?) at the *entreaty* of the Jewish converts, and, as
St. Epiphanius relates, commissioned by the apostles.
He wrote his gospel whilst he was in Judea or
Palestine, and that in Hebrew, or Syro-Chaldaic,
which the Jews in Palestine spoke at that time. St.
Bartholomew took a copy of it with him into India
and left it there; but it was brought back to Alexandria
by St. Pantænus, who had gone thither, and returned
to the said city about the year 200. St. Jerome says,
that he saw a copy of this gospel in the original

Hebrew in the library at Cæsarea.* The original is
not now extant, but as it was translated into Greek,
in the time of the apostles, that version was of equal
authority; for, the Syro-Chaldaic copy seems to have
been soon corrupted by the Nazareans, or Jewish
converts, who adhered to the ceremonies of the law.
Also the Ebionite heretics retrenched many passages.
Their interpolations and falsifications brought the
Hebrew copy into disrepute in the Church.

This gospel, being the first in order, contains also
the first and most important rule of faith, showing
thereby, that the gospel itself cannot be held as such.

The Church of Christ was to be like a city on the
mountain, and as firmly established thereon, as it
was to be visible to mankind; we therefore see
(xvi. 16) our Saviour addressing St. Peter:—" And I
say to thee, that thou art Peter, and upon this rock
will I build My Church, and the gates of hell shall
not prevail against her." This Church, governed and
guided by pastors, we find further exalted and pointed
out to us, as our rule in faith and morals, in xviii. 17,
where our Saviour says:—" And if he will not hear
them, tell the CHURCH, (which is: the pastors); and
if he will not hear *the Church*, let him be as an
heathen, and as a publican."

These texts so incontestibly establish a visible
Church of Christ, and her superior authority in her
pastors, as they do likewise establish the heinous
guilt of separating from and disobeying her, that the
so-called Reformers, the followers of the Nazareans
and Ebionites, wilfully corrupted them, in order to
cover and gloss over their wicked rebellion against

---

* In the Cathedral of Vercelli is shown an old manuscript
copy of the gospels of St. Matthew and St. Mark, said to
be written by St. Eusebius, bishop of that place, who died
A.D. 371. It was almost worn out with age near 800 years
ago, when King Berengarius caused it to be covered with
plates of silver.

the Church, and their separation therefrom; they also, by these intentional corruptions, wished to blind the people, and to make them believe that Christ instituted neither a Church to whom they *distinctively* ought to belong and adhere, nor pastors to whom they were to submit in matters of religion. They tried to effect this by substituting not only in the above two texts, but all throughout the Bible, the word "congregation" for that of "Church;" they made our blessed Redeemer say:—"upon this rock will I build my congregation;" "tell the congregation, and if he will not hear the congregation;" and notwithstanding these falsifications, these men are venerated as clearheaded Reformers, as the virtuous and learned restorers of religious truth! Was there ever a people more imposed upon than their followers?

The above, as well as other corruptions, pervaded the whole Bible; and upon this corrupted foundation, the fabric of Protestantism, but particularly that of the Established Church, has been raised. That a building, erected, not upon pillars of truth, but upon the rotten pillars of falsehood, cannot stand, is as certain and palpable, as that no later correction of the sacred text can wipe away its corrupted and illegitimate parentage. And Christ should adopt such an offspring as His own? The Established Church of England has certified its impure origin; has put its seal upon the fact of being, not the work of God, but the creature of wicked men, by correcting the aforesaid falsification, which for nearly a hundred years it had propagated, knowingly too, *as the word of God.* Instead of the "Church" of Christ, we find the Protestant "congregation" throughout the first Protestant Bibles, printed in 1534, 1539, 1562, 1577, 1579, and in the Genevan of 1557, until the word "Church" was restored again in place of "congregation" in the translation of 1611, which is the present *authorised* (by whom?) version. The restoration of the word "Church" has unfortunately not restored the dissenting "congregation" of England to the Church of Christ, which it left under false and simulated colours ; it has served, on the contrary, more clearly to vindicate and manifest the true rule of faith, which, according to St. Matthew, our Saviour mercifully gave us :—" Hear the Church," but not, on any account, one that is guilty of, and founded upon, a wilfully CORRUPTED GOSPEL.

2.—THE GOSPEL OF ST. MARK.

St. Mark, the disciple and interpreter of St. Peter, (saith St. Jerome), according to what he had *heard* from Peter himself, wrote at Rome a brief gospel, about the year of Christ 43, or 10 years after our Lord's ascension, (why ?) at the *request of the converts there*, who, as Eusebius relates, (book ii. chap. xiv.), not content to have *heard* St. Peter *preaching, pressed* St. Mark to pen an historical account of what the Prince of the Apostles had *delivered to them by word of mouth*. St. Peter rejoiced at the affection of the faithful, revised the work, and gave it his approbation, that *with his authority* (without which it would not have been received) it might be publicly read in the religious assemblies of the Church. Hence it might be, that, as we learn from Tertullian, some attributed this gospel to St. Peter himself. The last chapter was doubted by some ancient writers. Baronius and others say, that the original was written in Latin, but the more general opinion is, that the evangelist wrote it in Greek. An old manuscript of this gospel is kept in St. Mark s treasury at Venice, and is *there said to be* the original copy, written by the evangelist himself; but the learned antiquarians have forgotten to say, as far as we can find, whether it is written in Greek or Latin. It was conveyed from Aquileja to Venice in the fifteenth century. The Emperor Charles IV. in 1355, obtained from Aquileja the last eight leaves, which are kept at Prague. The twenty leaves at

Venice, with the last eight leaves at Prague, make the whole gospel of St. Mark, which belongs to the other three gospels in the Forojulian MS. This MS was written in the sixth century, and contains the oldest copy of St. Jerome's version of the gospels.

It is evident from what has been said, that this gospel was not written as a rule of faith; like the others, however, it contains THE rule established by our divine Redeemer, in His charge to the apostles:—
"*Go ye into the whole world and* PREACH *the gospel to every creature.*" (xvi. 15.)

3.—THE GOSPEL OF ST. LUKE.

St. Luke was a native of Antioch, the capital of Syria: he was by profession a physician, and some ancient writers say, that he was very skilful in painting. He was converted by St Paul, and became his disciple and companion in his travels, and fellow-labourer in the ministry of the gospel. He wrote in Greek, about 24 years after our Lord's ascension, (why?) partly to expose the false and fabulous relations which already began to be obtruded upon the world, as we learn from the first verse of his first chapter; partly, as some imagine, (though it does not clearly appear that he had read them, as Calmet and others observe), to supply what seemed wanting in St. Matthew and St. Mark, relating several facts and discourses, as also the reasons and occasions for many things being done or spoken, wholly omitted by them. He writes from *tradition*, (as we learn *from himself*, in the second verse of his first chapter), not from necessity, but simply, according to the next verse, (why?) because it *seemed* good to him, and only, according to the fourth verse, in order that his friend and disciple, Theophilus, might know the *verity*, the *certainty*, of those words, of those things in which he *had already verbally* been instructed. He moreover simply writes, not to his flock, or any other flock, or to the Church at large, but to *one* beloved disciple ; not to give him a *complete* history of the life of our Saviour, still less a rule of faith ; but exclusively, in order to ground him yet more firmly and with certainty in those things which he, Theophilus, *knows already from hearing.*

Some part of the 22d chapter was doubted by ancient writers, and the gospel itself, as also the others, denied by one or the other of primitive and modern heretics.

4.—THE GOSPEL OF ST JOHN.

St. John, the apostle, evangelist, and prophet, was the son of Zebedee and Salome, and brother to James the Greater. He was called the *beloved disciple of Christ*, and stood by at His crucifixion. He wrote the gospel after the other evangelists, (why ?) at the *importunity*, as St. Jerome says, of the Asian bishops, about 63 years after our Lord's ascension. Many things that they had omitted were supplied by him. The original was written in Greek, and by the Greeks he is entitled the *Divine*, or Theologian. When, according to St. Jerome, he was *earnestly requested* by the brethren to write the gospel ; he answered he would do it, if, by ordering a *common fast*, they would all put up their prayers together to the Almighty God ; which being ended, replenished with the clearest and fullest revelation, he burst forth into that preface :—" In the beginning was the word," &c.

We here see, that, no more than the other evangelists, did St. John write from necessity, or with the object of making his gospel a rule of faith. He speaks (xxi. 25) of THINGS that are *not written*, and (xx. 30, 31), of SIGNS—not of doctrines, not of his gospel to be a rule of faith—but of SIGNS that *are written*, that we might believe in Christ ; and believing in Christ is, to hear Him, to hear the apostles :—" He that heareth you, heareth Me ;" and to hear the apostles is, to hear those whom they commanded to teach and to be obeyed, namely; the prelates and pastors of the Church.

Some ancient writers doubted the beginning of the eighth chapter of this gospel.

5.—THE ACTS OF THE APOSTLES.

This book, whose very title proclaims its character and nature, and which from the first ages has been called (not a rule of faith, but) the *Acts of the Apostles*, is not to be considered as a history of what was done by *all* the apostles, who were dispersed among different nations; but only *a short view, a record, of the first establishment of the Christian Church*. A part of the preaching and actions of St. Peter are related in the first twelve chapters, and a particular account of St. Paul's apostolical labours in the subsequent chapters. It was written by St. Luke the evangelist, (why?) not as a rule of faith, nor as a review, a statement and explanation of the doctrines of Christianity; it was only, as we have seen above, a short account of the first years of the Church, written not to any flock of his, much less to the Church at large, but, like his gospel narrative, to and for his friend and disciple Theophilus alone, as we learn from the first verse of his first chapter. This record of St. Luke, as we likewise learn from the verse just quoted, being a continuation of his gospel, its narration commences at the ascension of our Lord, and ends in the year 63, when he finished these acts at Rome, (St. Paul being liberated from prison, where he had been kept two years), briefly embracing about 30 years of the history of the Church. The original was written in Greek.

This part of the New Testament, almost on every page, contains the rule of faith, which our Saviour, as well as the apostles, laid down, and upon which they acted, namely; *preaching and teaching*. However, to convert it likewise into an instrument of perdition instead of salvation; to make it also answer their hypocritical declamations against the Catholic Church: there is hardly any corruption of the Bible, on the part of the audacious and shameless Deformers, more wicked than that which they wilfully effected in the 9th chapter, the 22nd verse. This verse, the Catholic version gives as follows:—"But Saul increased much more in strength, and confounded the Jews who dwelt at Damascus, affirming that this is the Christ." The instruments of the powers of darkness gave to this verse the following turn:—"Saul confounded the Jews, proving, *by conferring one Scripture with another*, that this is very Christ." And branding with infamy their predecessors, the founders of their communion, their spiritual parents: the authorities of the Established Church corrected it in their last translation, in which this verse now stands as follows: —"But Saul increased the more in strength, and confounded the Jews which dwelt at Damascus, proving that this is very Christ."

Alas! no correction of a polluted Bible can change Satan into an angel, can blot out the illegitimate birth and ungodly character of Protestantism and the Established Church; no act of parliament can make divine, though it may proclaim so, an institution with the mark of adulteration of the word of God on its forehead. Alas! it is enough to shed tears over the delusion, in which the wickedness, hypocrisy, and ignorance (in many unconscious) of the leaders of the Protestant Church have held, and still hold, this once favoured nation.

The aforesaid corruption, a pure and wilful addition to the holy word of God, making it the word of the devil, found in the Bible of 1577, was made in favour of the *presumptive opinion*, that the comparing of Scriptures is enough for any man to understand them himself, solely by his own diligence and endeavour; and thereby to reject both the commentaries of the doctors, the exposition of holy councils, and the Catholic Church, the latter of which alone you will find your only true and faithful guide to salvation. No lie proceeded yet from the Church of God; why, then, not believe her? Why follow still the again and again self-conceited falsificators of the word of God and their successors? Do you believe them more faithful, more competent, in the delivery of the unwritten than they have proved themselves in the written word? Are you sure whether they teach you true or false? And can *you* judge of it?

Dear Protestant reader, do not *risk your eternal salvation; think, think, think but a little* whence your religion comes, and whether our blessed Saviour can look upon it as His child. See, He has but one ark; He rides still in the bark of Peter; Pius IX. is at the helm; come and join his millions of faithful.

6.—THE EPISTLE OF ST. PAUL THE APOSTLE TO THE ROMANS.

St. Paul wrote this epistle at Corinth, when he was preparing to go to Jerusalem with the charitable contributions collected in Achaija and Macedonia for the relief of the Christians in Judea; which was about 24 years after our Lord's ascension. It was written in Greek, but, at the same time, translated into Latin, for the benefit of those who did not understand the former language; and though it is not the first of his epistles in the order of time, yet it is first placed, on account of the sublimity of the matter it contains, and of the *preeminence* of the place to which it was sent, and in veneration of the Church.

As the parent pens his most affectionate letters to the best of his children; as the friend pours out his most elevated thoughts and sentiments to that friend whose heart is most like his own; as there is an ineffable desire on the part of faithful, virtuous, and loving souls, always to commune with each other, personally, or if absent, by letter: so St. Paul, the loving and undaunted champion of Christ, longed to commune with the faithful of Rome, "whose faith," like his own, "was spoken of in the whole world." (i. 8.) This ardent longing (i. 11,) after those in whom he saw his own faith reflected, caused him to write this epistle—but not with the wish or intention to give them a history of Christ, to lay down for them a rule of faith, nay, not even to teach them the duties of that divine religion which he preached; for, from *hearing*, they knew and practised all this long since, "for, their faith was already spoken of in the *whole world*."

This appears further, when he writes (xvi. 17,) to his beloved Romans: "Now I beseech you, brethren, to mark them who make dissensions and offences contrary to the doctrines (not, which he had written, or was still writing to them, but) which you HAVE *learnt;*" for, there was no teaching doctrines to those "whose faith was spoken of at the time in the whole world." St. Paul so far gives the Romans, and of course to all the faithful, a rule of faith (and would to God it had always been practised by the laity!) as to request, to *beseech* them, *not to follow any dissenters;* and what else were *all those who fell from the Catholic Church,* but such as made dissensions? Mark it well, dear reader; it is the Apostle Paul who says:—*No dissent;* nay, *no dissent even from the Roman Church,* since then grown up from infancy into the vigour of manhood, still the *same Roman Church.*

7.—THE FIRST EPISTLE OF ST. PAUL TO THE CORINTHIANS.

St Paul having planted the faith in Corinth, where he had preached a year and a half, and converted a great many, went to Ephesus. After being there three years, he wrote this first epistle to the Corinthians, and sent it by the same persons, Stephanas,

Fortunatus, and Achaicus, who had brought their letter to him. It was written in Greek, about 24 years after our Lord's ascension, and contains several matters appertaining to faith and morals, and also to ecclesiastical discipline.

That this epistle was written, not as a code, nor part of it, of Christian doctrine, but simply as instructions, reproofs, and admonitions, necessarily interspersed with doctrinal points, is manifest throughout the whole of it. The only necessity of its being written at all was, the unavoidable absence of the apostle from his former flock, who had learned from him *all doctrine* by his *verbal teaching* and by *their hearing;* the epistle is no repetition, no rehearsing of what St. Paul had verbally taught them.

Being no rule of faith itself, this epistle nevertheless contains a *most important one*. As the pastor of an undivided Church, one, holy, catholic, and apostolic, he writes to one of her branches, in active and undivided communion with all the others, in order that "they should all speak the *same thing*, that there should be *no schisms* amongst them." (i. 10.) It has been signified to him, he continues, "that every one of you saith: I indeed am of Paul: and I am of Apollo: and I of Cephas: and I of Christ. Is Christ (or His Church) divided? Was Paul then crucified for you? or were you baptised in the name of Paul?" (i. 11, 12, 13.) This very Paul, and with him the voice of the whole Catholic Church, of which he was a pillar, address themselves to all those who would fain make the Church of Christ consist of all sorts of denominations; to you, my dear readers, they address themselves; for they hear you say: "I indeed am of Luther: and I am of Calvin: and I am of Zwingli: and I of the Established Church of Henry VIII. and Queen Elizabeth: and I of Wesley, or God knows of whom." Is Christ, *is His Church divided?* Was Luther crucified for you? Were you baptised in his name? or in that of Calvin? or in that of any other separatist? When, thus, *contentions within* the Church are so severely rebuked by St. Paul, how will he not, and how does he not actually anathematize *dissensions from the Church!*—Let this rule sink deeply into your mind, dear Protestant reader.

8.—THE SECOND EPISTLE OF ST. PAUL TO THE CORINTHIANS.

In this epistle St. Paul comforts those who are now reformed by his admonitions to them in the former one, and *absolves the incestuous man on doing penance*, whom he had before *excommunicated* for his crime. Hence he treats of true penance, and of *the dignity of the ministers of the New Testament*. He cautions the faithful against *false teachers*, and the society of infidels. He gives an account of his sufferings, and also of the favours and graces which God has bestowed upon him. This second epistle was written in the same year with the first, also in Greek, like all his writings, and sent, by Titus, from some place in Macedonia.

It is hardly necessary—it would be an insult to the most moderate understanding—further to notice why this epistle was written, or to show that it was not to be an exclusive, nor part of any exclusive rule of faith. St. Paul, in fact, absolutely declares the why and wherefore of his writing (xiii. 16):—"*Therefore* I write these things BEING ABSENT, that being present (when he would again be with them), I may not *deal more severely*, according to the power which the Lord has given me unto edification." One positive rule of faith, however, he gives, which is, the *avoidance of false teachers;* who need but teach something new, something not previously heard of in the Church, in order to be known as the messengers of any one but Christ. Look then about you,—not for doctrine or discipline that may please you, but for *true and faithful teachers!*

9.—THE EPISTLE OF ST. PAUL TO THE GALATIANS.

The Galatians, soon after St. Paul had *preached* the gospel to them, were seduced by some false teachers, who had been Jews, and who were for obliging all Christians, even those who had been Gentiles, to observe circumcision and the other ceremonies of the Mosaical law. In this epistle he refutes the pernicious doctrine of these teachers, and also their calumny against his mission and apostleship. Its subject matter is much the same as in that to the Romans. It was written at Ephesus about 23 years after our Lord's ascension.

Respecting the character of this epistle as a rule of faith, or as a rehearsal of what St. Paul had taught the Galatians, there can but still less be the question as of the Epistles to the Corinthians; for, as St. Paul says, (i. 8, 9):—"But though we, (even himself) or an angel from heaven, preach a gospel to you *besides* that which we *have preached* to you (already), let him be anathema." If his epistle were to have served as *something like* a rule of faith, the apostle would not have said, (vi. 11):—"See what a (long) *letter* I have written to you with my own hand."

As noticed in the remarks on the preceding epistle, a doctrine to be false need but to be new. If it was necessary for St. Paul, for the performance of his ministry, to be received and acknowledged by the apostles (Acts ix. 26, 27); if, again, it was necessary "for James, Cephas (Peter) and John, who seemed to be pillars, to *approve of his teaching*, and to give him the right hand of fellowship," (Gal. ii. 9): how can his *writings*, so hard to be understood, and which the unlearned and the unstable wrest to their destruction, be a rule of faith, without some *lawful authority*, to *approve of their explanation?* And how can those national or local churches (if they deserve such a name) belong to the true Church, who, unlike St. Paul, have not only no sort of fellowship with the

Church of Peter, but not even fellowship with one another? Whose *first*, and of course succeeding ministers were neither, like St. Paul by St. Peter, approved of by the successors of the Prince of the Apostles, of St. James, and St. John, nor acknowledged by the Church they seceded from? Let this then be your rule of faith: that those who have no communion, no fellowship with the Church of Peter,* are false teachers, and as such to be avoided; men that teach *profane novelties*, widely different from what has been delivered to them, widely different from what St. Paul had *received* and *delivered* to the Galatians; and who, therefore, if even they were angels from heaven instead of messengers from another place, fall under the curse of the Apostle of the Gentiles. Beware, then, of the apostates from the Catholic Church, or of the institutions, or rather sects, they may have founded.

10.—THE EPISTLE OF ST. PAUL TO THE EPHESIANS.

Ephesus was the capital of Lesser Asia, and celebrated for the temple of Diana, to which the greater part of the people of the East went frequently to worship. But St. Paul having preached the gospel there for two years the first time, and afterwards about a year, he converted many. He wrote this epistle to them when he was a prisoner in Rome, and sent it by Tychicus. He admonishes them to hold firmly the *faith which they had received*, (v. 13), and warns them, and also those of the neighbouring cities, against the sophistry of philosophers, and the doctrine of *false teachers*, who had come among them. The matters of faith in this epistle are exceedingly sublime, and consequently very difficult to be understood. It was written about 29 years after our Lord's ascension.

* Those visible members of an invisible church, those visible branches of an invisible tree.

That neither this epistle, nor the sacred writings taken all together, are a rule, or *the* rule of faith, or a means even of perfection, without the assistance and instructions of lawfully *appointed*, not self-elected, or by the people elected, teachers, is most clearly and abundantly proved in this very epistle: for St. Paul says, (iv. 11, 12, 13):—And *He* gave some apostles, and some prophets, and other some evangelists, and other some pastors and doctors (but no Bible), for the *perfecting of the saints*, for the *work of the ministry*, for the edifying of the body of Christ (which is His Church): until we all meet in the *unity of faith* (not by means of the Bible) and of the knowledge of the Son of God," &c. St. Paul wants the prayers of the faithful, (vi. 19,) to enable him, not to write but "to *open his mouth* with confidence to *make known the mystery of the gospel.*" And that the Ephesians may know *all things* (for he has written but little, and this little no rule of faith): Tychicus, the *faithful* minister in the Lord (appointed by St. Paul) will make known to you all things." "Whom I HAVE SENT to you *for this purpose*," &c. (vi. 21, 22.)

Thus, the *faithful* ministers, the apostles, prophets, evangelists, pastors, and doctors of the Church, are your rule of faith; follow, therefore, the apostle's advice, and seek no true faith in the *faithless* ministers of the Church, nor in their *faithless* copies and translations of the sacred writings. The Church cannot become *faithless* to Christ, because she is the pillar and ground of truth, with whom He promised to remain unto the end of the world.

False teachers, of whom we are so often warned to beware, must either spring up without the Church, or they must spring up within, *fall away from*, and become *faithless* to her, as St. Paul has it, (Gal. i. 7): —" Only there are *some* (not the Church) that trouble you, and would *pervert* the gospel of Christ;" and as he says to Tim. (1, iv. 1):—" SOME (not the Church(shall *depart from the faith,*" and thus become *faithless* to the Church. And was not this the case with every so-called Reformer since the time of the apostles? Was *any one* of them *faithful to the Church? faithful to his vows to God? faithful* to the doctrines that had been *delivered to him? faithful* to the doctrines he had *preached already?* Were they not all *faithless ministers*, instead of *faithful?* Were they not *all faithless in all.*

And in this epistle, as in the gospel of St. Matthew, by becoming *faithless* to the Church, *which is the body of Christ*, they became faithless also to the written word of God. Not content with their own perdition, they must needs also confirm the people in the abandonment of the ancient faith, from which at first they had been forced to fall, by effacing from the Bible the name of "Church," and, as we have seen already, substituting that of "congregation." We dwell again upon this particular corruption, to show the barefaced, the inconceivable malignity, in thus wilfully falsifying the word of God, as will be evident to every one comparing the following texts:—

The true English, according to the Rhemish translation.	Corruptions in the Protestant Bibles, printed A.D. 1562, 1577, 1579; as also in Tyndall's, 1534, and Cranmer's, 1539.	The last translation of the English Protestant Bible of 1611.
Ephes. Husbands, love, ver. 23, your wives, as 24, 25, Christ loved the 27, 29, "church."—ver. 32. 25.	Husbands love your wives, as Christ loved the "congregation."	Corrected.
That he might present to himself a glorious "church."-ver. 27.	That he might present to himself a glorious "congregation"	Corrected.
For this is a great "sacrament," but I speak in Christ and in the "church."-ver. 32.	For this is a great "secret," for I speak in Christ, and in the "congregation."	This is a great "mystery," but I speak concerning Christ and "the church."

Chap. i. And hath made 22, 23, him head over all the "church" *which is his body,* the fulness of him "which is filled" all in all.	And gave him to be the head over all things to the "congregation," which is his body, the fulness of him "that filleth" all in all.	And gave him to be the head over all things to the "church," which is his body, the fulness of him that "filleth" all in all.

These glaring and flagrant violations of the sacred Scriptures having been condemned and corrected in the said edition of 1611, after the "dissenting *congregation* of England" had obtained the semblance of a Church, this seeming phantom of the body of Christ has, in these particular instances, again partly become faithful to the letter of the written word of God, but not to the spirit of it; and her first faithlessness to the Church, her first and chief infidelity still remains.

By the subsequent corrections of the wilful falsifications of the Bible, by the *lights* of the Reformation, the Church of Christ, as the rule of faith, has been but more exalted, as well as the scrupulosity with which she ever has been, and still is, the guardian of both the unwritten and the written word of God.

The doctrinal corruption in the above-cited verse 32, where the word "secret," instead of the word "sacrament, has been placed, and its later alteration into the word "mystery," as it stands at present, will not escape the sincere and attentive reader; he will, with the grace of God, be able to judge which is the most trustworthy and the safest rule of faith.

11.—THE EPISTLE OF ST. PAUL TO THE PHILIPPIANS.

The Philippians were the first among the Macedonians converted to the faith. They had a great veneration for St. Paul, and supplied his wants when he was a prisoner in Rome, sending to him by Epaphroditus, by whom he sent this epistle, in which he recommends charity, *unity,* and humility, and warns them against *false teachers,* whom he calls *dogs*,* and enemies of the cross of Christ. He also returns thanks for their benefactions. It was written about 29 years after our Lord's ascension; and, in writing it, he did not, according to the first verse of the third chapter, "find the task wearisome to him," because he was doing good; it being *necessary for them* (owing to St. Paul's absence) to be warned against *false teachers*.

The rule of faith therein implied is: that, being ware of false teachers, they should not have recourse to his epistle, or to Scripture, as their guide to salvation, but to *true teachers*, to those *faithful pastors and doctors* of St. Paul, who, with their *faithful flocks*, from the Church, the undivided body of Christ. The apostle does not send his epistle to the Philippians as their way to heaven, but as *necessary* to warn them against *false teachers;* whilst, on the other hand, he makes it serve, at the same time, as the *letter of credence* of a *true teacher:*—"having thought it *necessary* to send you Epaphroditus my brother and fellow-labourer and fellow-soldier, but *your apostle*, and he that hath ministered to my wants." (ii. 25.(

Not only the New Testament, but the whole Bible, has in this manner been delivered to all nations, by the *faithful* pastors of the Catholic Church, as was this epistle by Epaphroditus to the Philippians; not as a rule of faith, but rather as a beacon, to warn them likewise against false teachers, and also as letters of credence of *their own apostleship and true teaching*. In the hands of Protestant reformers, having received the Bible from the Catholic Church, it is like the stolen letter of introduction,—like the stolen passport in the hand of a dishonest stranger; who, not finding therein either birth-place, parentage, name, age, stature, livery, profession, or character, or any other

---

* Protestants would be very angry, if St. Paul were to apply that word to the convicted adulterators of the Scriptures—to the founders of the miscalled Reformation.

distinctive mark of recognition or identification, agree with his own person and condition, goes and effects erasures and forgeries, to make it answer his evil inclinations and purposes.

12.—THE EPISTLE OF ST PAUL TO THE COLOSSIANS.

Colossa was a city of Phrygia, near Laodicea. It does not appear that St. Paul preached there himself, but that the Colossians were converted (not by the Bible, but by tradition) by the *preaching* and *teaching* of Epaphras, (i. 7), a disciple of the apostles. However, as St. Paul was the great apostle of the Gentiles, he wrote this epistle to the Colossians, when he was in prison, and about the same time that he wrote to the Ephesians and Philippians. The exhortations and doctrine it contains are similar to that which is set forth in his epistle to the Ephesians, and, like this, serves as *a letter of credence* of the bearers :—"Tychicus, (iv. 7, 8, 9), our dearest brother, and *faithful* minister, whom I have sent to you for this same purpose, that he may know the things that concern you, and *comfort your hearts*, with Onesimus, a most beloved and *faithful brother*, who is one of you. *All things* that are done here, THEY shall make known to you."

The instruction given by St Paul to Tychicus and Onesimus, to read among, or to the Colossians, the epistle they had to deliver, and which was also to be read in the neighbouring city of Laodicea, has always been and is still followed by the Catholic Church, portions of the Gospels and Epistles being read to the congregations every Sunday. The Colossians were to receive the two ambassadors (not the epistle) to hear from them all things, to be comforted by them, in the same manner as the nations of the earth were to receive the lawful successors of these ambassadors, accompanied by the sacred volume; the nations of the earth could no more seize upon the hallowed book, explain it at their pleasure, and discard the ministers who brought it, than the Colossians could in a similar manner have opposed themselves to the teaching and authority of the messengers of St. Paul.

These apostolic messengers, or missionaries, necessarily taught *from tradition; they, as pastors* of the then already Catholic Church, were the rule of faith, and not the epistle which they carried. However, to throw discredit on the Church, and on her authoritative traditionary teaching; to discard her as THE guide to salvation, Protestants here, also, in their wilful, and partly, *perhaps*, (though *Reformers!*) ignorant corruption of the Bible, have substituted the words:— "ordinances," "instruction," for that of "tradition," wherever it militated against them; and moreover, wherever they were able, to cast a stigma on this word, they were sure to do so to suit their own purpose. In this epistle, for instance, (ii. 20), the Catholic version is as follows:—

"If, then, you be dead with Christ from the 'elements' of this world, why do you yet 'decree' as living in the world?"

In the Protestant Bible of 1579, the same verse is given this way:—

"If 'ye' be dead with Christ from the 'rudiments' of 'the' world, why, 'as though' living in the world, 'are ye led with traditions?'"

And in another Protestant Bible, as in that of Geneva of 1557, the latter part of this text runs thus:

"Are ye burthened with traditions?"

And in the last Protestant translation it is:—

"Are you subject to ordinances?"

Now, in the Greek text of this verse, there is no word signifying "tradition;" and this intentional falsification is even acknowledged by the correction in the edition of 1683, where the word "ordinances" has been substituted for that of "tradition." There can thus be no question, that:—"why, as though

living in the world, *are ye led with traditions?"*—
"are ye burthened with traditions?"—were made use
of, to make the very word tradition, as it is to this
day among uninformed Protestants, odious among
the people.

Are these misnamed Reformers, these falsifiers of
the word of life; are these soul-destroyers your Gods,
your apostles? my dear Protestant fellow-christians!
Awake from your deception, cling to that rule of
faith, to that divinely instituted Church, whom her
worst enemies have *never* charged with the corruption,
but highly praised, as you will see, for the pure preservation of the sacred writings! And if these sacred
writings, far more easily corrupted than universal
public teaching; if these have been kept by her,
undefiled, for the space of 1800 years, she must surely
be the true and sole rule of faith, the Church of the
living God, the body of Christ, the pillar and ground
of truth!

13.—THE FIRST EPISTLE OF ST. PAUL TO THE THESSALONIANS.

Thessalonia was the capital of Macedonia, in which
St. Paul having preached the gospel, converted some
Jews and a great number of the Gentiles: but the
unbelieving Jews, envying his success, raised such a
commotion against him, that he and his companion
Sylvanus were obliged to quit the city. He afterwards went to Athens, where he heard that the converts in Thessalonia were under a severe persecution
ever since his departure, and lest they should lose
their fortitude, he sent Timothy to strengthen and
comfort them in their suffering. In the meantime,
St. Paul came to Corinth, where he wrote this first
epistle, and also the second to the Thessalonians,
both in the same year, being the 19th after our Lord's
ascension. These are the first of the epistles in the
order of time.

Respecting the charge of St. Paul in the present epistle, (v. 28), "that it be read *to* (not *by*) all the holy brethren:" the same as has been said in regard to the preceding epistle to the Colossians, is applicable here also. The epistle alone would not have done for the Thessalonians; but, (iii. 2): *we sent Timothy* our brother, and the minister of God in the gospel of Christ, to *confirm* you (in what they knew already from *hearing*) and exhort you (they were to *hear* still more) *concerning your faith.*" They were, moreover, to *hear* (v. 27), the epistle *read;* not, to read, much less to explain or interpret it themselves.

14.—THE SECOND EPISTLE OF ST. PAUL TO THE THESSALONIANS.

In this epistle, St. Paul admonishes the Thessalonians to be constant in the faith of Christ, and not to be terrified by the *insinuations of false teachers*, telling them that the day of judgment was not near at hand, as there must come many signs and wonders before it. He bids them (ii. 14), "to hold firm the *traditions*, received from him, whether by word, or by epistle;" and shows them, how they may be certain of his letters by the manner he writes in. As to its being no rule of faith, the epistle speaks for itself; but it exhibits in a most beautiful and clear manner the true rule of faith of the Church of God, viz.: the word of God, whether written or unwritten. For this reason then, also, the Reformers did not fail, in the corruption of their hearts, to corrupt again the words of life, in this particular instance, that they might give a stab to the Church, and a blow to her traditional teaching. This they accomplished, as we have seen already, by substituting "ordinances" for "traditions;" and in iii. 6, where the word "traditions" likewise occurs, they substituted "instructions;" and all this they did, to suit their desertion from the Church, whose traditions they would no longer follow.

In Tyndall's Bible of 1534, and Cranmer's of 1539, "institution" was placed for "tradition." However, the latter word was restored in the edition of 1611, thus adding one more proof in favour of the veracity and purity of the teaching of the Catholic Church; one more self-crimination to the many others, of Protestantism being the offspring of the father of lies and hypocrisy. Alas! for the quantity and quality of cockle sown among the wheat of Christ, by men considered as *Reformers*, as *peculiarly enlightened!*

15.—THE FIRST EPISTLE OF ST. PAUL TO TIMOTHY.

St. Paul writes this epistle to his *beloved Timothy*, being then Bishop of Ephesus, to instruct him in the duties of a bishop, both in respect to himself and to his charge; and that he ought to be well informed of the good morals of those on whom he was to impose hands: "Impose not hands lightly upon any man." He tells him also how he should behave towards his clergy. This epistle was written about 33 years after our Lord's ascension; but where it was written is uncertain; the more general opinion is, that it was in Macedonia.

The fact of this epistle being addressed to a pastor of the Church, and moreover to a bishop, precludes it at once from being—were it even so for the clergy —a rule of faith for the laity, by them to be tortured into all sorts of meanings.

That verbal, traditional teaching, was the rule of the Church, is shown in i. 3: "That thou mightest charge some not to *teach* otherwise." St. Paul does not write a *rule of faith* to Timothy, for he says, (iii. 14, 16): "These things I write to thee, *hoping that I shall come to thee shortly.* But if I tarry long, that thou mayest know (not articles of faith and doctrine, but(*how thou oughtest to behave thyself in the house of God*, which is the Church of the living God, the *pillar and ground of truth.*"

Thus, speaking of the *Church of the living God*, as the pillar and ground of truth, St. Paul points her out to us as the *visible* and *audible* rule of faith; but to cast off this *Church* of the living God, the so-called Reformers, here as in other places, substituted the word "congregation" for that of "Church," saying: "The house of God, which is the *'congregation'* of the living God," &c.;—a *congregation* the pillar and ground of truth!!

On one occasion our Saviour told his apostles: "He that heareth you, heareth me, he that despiseth you, despiseth me, and he that despiseth me, despiseth Him that sent me." That this declaration was not to lose its force until the end of the world, but was to remain valid in the persons of the successors of the apostles, in the persons of those forming the *faithful and united priesthood of the Catholic Church*, forming her *living voice*, we find in the following charge of St. Paul to Timothy, (iv. 11, 12): "These things *command* and *teach*. Let no man *despise* thy youth," &c.; and further, as if to remind him of the elevated position he occupied in the Church of Christ, and to proclaim the spiritual, the superior power of her priesthood, the apostle continues to exhort him, (ver. 14): "Neglect not the *grace* that is in thee, which is given thee by prophecy, with imposition of the hands of the *priesthood*." As, however, neither Church, nor priesthood, nor authority—not to be despised even in a youth—was palatable to men who forsook them, who, like the calumniators of St. Paul, spoken of at page 29, slandered their spiritual mother, disgraced holy orders, and rebelled against those who had the rule over them, despising both the one and the other; so it was also to be expected, that they would not spare, would not neglect to falsify the word of God, in order to make good in the eyes of a defrauded people, their wicked apostacy from the spouse of Christ. Besides the corruption (now corrected) pointed out above, the verse just quoted was rendered as follows, in the Bibles of 1562, 1577, and 1579: "Neglect not the *gift* that is in thee, which was given thee by prophecy, with the laying on of the hands of the eldership." Tyndall's Bible of 1534 had it: "gift"—"of an elder;" Cranmer's Bible of 1539, had it: "gift"—"laying on of the hands by authority of priesthood;" and the Geneva Bible of 1557 had it: "gift"— "with the laying on of the hands, by the eldership."

It is left to the reader to judge, why "gift" has been retained, instead of substituting for it "grace;" and why the *Greek* word "presbytery," and not the plain *English* word, "priesthood," has been substituted for "eldership."—A priesthood conferring grace, say gifts, if you please, exalts the Church of that priesthood, into a ruling authority, into a rule of faith; into true rulers not to be despised: and for this reason the English people are deluded by *Greek*, when English will not do.

That the people were to *hear* and to *obey* (in spiritual matters of course) that priesthood, that presbytery, if you like, of which St. Timothy was a member, we find again repeated by St. Paul's injunction, (vi 2): "These things *teach* and *exhort*."

Can the Church, and the authority of her priesthood be more prominently, more palpably pointed out as *the* rule of faith, than has been done by this epistle of St. Paul to Timothy?

16.—THE SECOND EPISTLE OF ST. PAUL TO TIMOTHY.

In this epistle the apostle again instructs and admonishes Timothy in what belonged to his office, as in the former; and also warns him to shun the conversation of those who had erred from the truth, describing at the same time their character. He tells him of his approaching death, and desires him to come speedily to him. It appears from this circumstance, that he wrote this second epistle in the time of his last imprisonment at Rome, and not long before

Banishing the very idea of a *written rule of faith*, St Paul does not say to Timothy: write carefully down all you have heard of me, but he tells him: "Hold the *form of sound words*, (not which I am and have been writing to you, but) which thou hast *heard* of me in 'faith, and in the love which is in Christ Jesus."—"Keep the good thing committed (not to a book, but) to *thy trust* by the Holy Ghost, who dwelleth in us." (ii. 13, 14.)—Neither does St. Paul tell him to write down any thing for posterity, to copy, or get his epistle to be copied, to compile a Bible and form Bible societies; but he tells him, (ii. 2): "And the things, which thou hast *heard* of me (not even does he include what he has *written* to him) by many witnesses, the same commend to faithful men, (not for them to propagate it by writing, but) who shall be fit to *teach* others also;"—from which it results moreover, that *succession of teaching* to the end of the world, requires also a *succession of lawfully appointed and faithful teachers.*

The holy Scriptures spoken of in iii. 15, has reference to the *Old Testament* alone; that they are no rule of faith, but only for bishops and pastors, in order to *teach*, or *reprove*, we have amply seen at page 11.

St. Paul's desiring Timothy to come speedily to him, was no doubt the real motive and occasion for his writing this epistle.

17.—THE EPISTLE OF ST PAUL TO TITUS.

St. Paul having preached the faith in the Island of Crete, he ordained his beloved disciple and companion bishop, and left him there to finish the work which he had begun. Afterwards the apostle, on a journey to Nicopolis, a city of Macedonia, wrote this epistle to Titus, in which he directs him to ordain *bishops and priests* for the different cities, showing him the principal qualities necessary for a bishop;

also gives him particular advice for his own conduct to his flock, exhorting him to hold to strictness of discipline, but seasoned with lenity. It was written 33 years after our Lord's ascension.

As was the case with Timothy, so here also St. Paul addresses a bishop under the same circumstances, bids him to appoint priests, (i. 5), the same as he (Titus), had been appointed by him, for the propagation of the gospel by word of mouth. There is here no question of a scriptural rule of faith; yet, if this epistle had been a rule of faith for Bishop Titus and the clergy, it was *their* business to *preach*, and to *explain* it to their flocks; but it was not permitted to the flock to explain it themselves, and by this rule to judge their clergy. The laity had and have to look only for *true* bishops, *true* pastors, *true* teachers, and for nothing else; these are their true rule of faith.

18.—THE EPISTLE OF ST. PAUL TO PHILEMON.

Philemon, a noble citizen of Colossa, had a servant named Onesimus, who had robbed him, and fled to Rome, where he met St. Paul, who was then a prisoner there for the first time. The apostle took compassion on him, and received him with tenderness, and converted him to the faith; for he was a Gentile before. St. Paul sends him back to his master, with this epistle in his favour; and though he beseeches Philemon to pardon him, yet the apostle writes with becoming dignity and authority. It contains divers profitable instructions, and points out the charity and humanity that masters should have for their servants.

That St. Paul did not mean this epistle to form a part or parcel of a rule of faith, nor that he wrote it for this reason, needs no demonstration.

19.—THE EPISTLE OF ST. PAUL TO THE HEBREWS.

St. Paul wrote this epistle to the Christians in Palestine, the greater part of whom being Jews before their conversion, they were called Hebrews. He exhorts them to be thoroughly converted and confirmed in the faith of Christ, clearly showing them the pre-eminence of Christ's priesthood over the Levitical, and also the excellence of the New Law above the Old. He commends faith by the example of the ancient fathers, and exhorts them to patience, and to perseverance, and to remain in fraternal charity. It appears from chapter xiii., that this epistle was written in Italy, and probably at Rome, about 29 years after our Lord's ascension.

That this epistle was not intended as a rule of faith, nor as part of one; that the Hebrews could not lawfully take any liberty with its text and explanation, is briefly settled by St. Paul himself, when he writes to them, and to all those who wish to be children of the Church:—"Remember *your prelates* who have *spoken* the word of God to you: *whose faith follow* considering the end of their conversation." (xii. 7.) "OBEY *your prelates*, and be SUBJECT to them." (xii. 17.) *Obedience and subjection, following the faith of the duly appointed pastors of the Church*, was the rule which, without any qualification, he positively enjoined to the Hebrews and to all the faithful; and it accords beautifully with the charge of our Saviour in the gospel of St. Matthew:—"Hear the Church."

Of "the Church of the firstborn," (ii. 23), the enlightened Reformers made "the congregation of the firstborn;" and in the editions of 1579 and 1580 they even presumed to strike St. Paul's name out of the very title of this epistle, therein following the heretic Marcion, who, as well as the Arians, denied it to be St. Paul's. Truly, the so-called Reformers did not "hear the Church!"

20.—THE CATHOLIC EPISTLE OF ST. JAMES THE APOSTLE.

This epistle is called *Catholic* or *Universal*, as formerly were also the two epistles of St. Peter, the first of St. John, and the one of St. Jude, because they were not written to any particular people or particular person, but to the faithful in general. It was written in Greek about the year 59 or after, more than 14 years after the death of St. James the Great, and a short time before his own martyrdom, by the apostle St. James the Less, who was also called the *brother of our Lord*, being his kinsman, (for cousins german with the Hebrews were called brothers). He was the first bishop of Jerusalem.

In this epistle are set forth many precepts appertaining to faith and morals ; and particularly, that faith without good works will not save a man, that true wisdom is given only from above. In the fifth chapter he publishes the sacrament of anointing the sick. Being addressed to the faithful in general, it might, as far as it goes, be taken as a rule of faith ; but, being also for this very reason pre-eminent above the rest of the gospels and epistles, which are addressed to individual bishops, congregations and laymen only, it is unfortunately much less considered and valued by Protestants, than these, both as regards good works, as well as the sacrament of extreme unction, which is not to be found in any Protestant persuasion. St. James referring (v. 14, 15 16), to the " elders,"—correctly translated, " the priests of the Church,"—precludes this epistle, like all the others, from being a rule of faith ; for, where there is a regularly and lawfully appointed priesthood, there can be no other rule of faith besides their preaching and teaching, *their explanation* of the written word of God. The misnamed Reformers, certainly, doing away with the Church, wished also to do away with the priesthood ; and thus, instead of saying with St. James, (v. 14) :—" let him bring in the 'priests' of the Church," they put :—" let him bring in the 'elders' of the congregation." In the edition of 1683, *the faithful* Protestant authorities became *faithless* to their own work, by transforming the " congregation" again into a "Church;" but they remained *faithful to the former corruption*, by not substituting "priest" for "elder," knowing, that there can be no priest, where, as in Protestant congregations or churches, there is no sacrifice. The perversion of *priest* into *elder*, strikes as well against the sacrifice of the new law, as against a divinely appointed priesthood, against the pastors of the Church, whom we were to hear. For this reason then also, *elder* is still put for *priest*, wherever the name or the word of priest appears, as of itself it is in favour of the Catholic Church; and thus the word of God is falsified, in order to efface, whatever tends to an acknowledgment of her existence and authority. This spirit was carried so far, that the two English Bibles of 1562 and 1577, usually read in the Protestant congregations, when they first were formed, had left out the word *catholic*, in the title of this, as well as of those other epistles, which have been known by the name of "Catholicæ Epistolæ" or "Catholic Epistles," ever since the apostles' time. (Euseb. Church History, book ii. chap. 23.) Their latter translations, dealing somewhat more honestly, have turned the word "Catholic" into "General;" "the General Epistle of James, of Peter, &c.," as if we should say in our creed,: "we believe the General Church;" and in asking for the *Catholic Church*, to ask for the *General Church!!!*

These, my dear Protestant fellow-christians,—these were the means to reconcile your forefathers to a false church or sect, and to a false rule of faith, after they had been forced from the *true* one.

This epistle was doubted by some ancient writers, and discredited (!!) by several of the Deformers.

21.—THE FIRST EPISTLE OF ST. PETER THE APOSTLE.

The first epistle of St. Peter, though brief, contains much doctrine concerning faith, hope, and charity, with divers instructions to all persons of what state or condition soever. The apostle commands submission to rulers and superiors, and exhorts all to the practice of a virtuous life in imitation of Christ. This epistle is written with such apostolical dignity, as to manifest the supreme authority, with which its writer, the Prince of the Apostles, had been vested by his Lord and master Jesus Christ. He wrote it at Rome, which figuratively he calls Babylon, about fifteen years after our Lord's ascension.

Like St. James and St. Paul, St. Peter gives us the rule of faith in a few words :—" Ancients, *feed* the flock of God which is among you," &c.; "neither lording it over the clergy, but being made a pattern of the flock from the heart." (v. 1, 2, 3.) "In like manner, ye young men, be *subject* to the ancients." (v. 5.) St. Peter here conveys, to the episcopal successors of the apostles, to the bishops of the Catholic Church, to the end of time, the same charge which he received from our Saviour :—" feed my lambs, feed my sheep ;" not only the laity, but even the clergy, are to be subject to the higher spiritual authority ; and if the clergy are to look up to the ancients, or bishops, for spiritual food, how much more necessary is it not for the laity to do so ? and if the flock of God is to be fed by the *living* voice of the pastors of the church, how can a dead book, the *dumb* and dead letter of the law, the written word of God, supply their place ? for again, faith comes from *hearing*, and the Bible can but be *read*, by those who have *learned* to read. St. Peter wrote :—" Ancients, *feed* the flock of God !" " Ye young men, be *subject* to the ancients," as if he imagined, that some time or other, by perverse children, the living rule would be exchanged for a dead one, because the former could and would not bend to their desires, whilst the dead rule might be applied according to their own pleasure and inclination. Therefore the command :—" Be subject to the *ancients*, of which *I also am one*;" thus exacting from the laity the same obedience to his *successors* and *fellow-pastors*, which he claimed to his own authority and teaching.

What an *unconditional obedience* does not St. Peter in this epistle, in this pastoral, enjoin here towards the "Church"—not towards the "congregation"—of Christ!

22.—THE SECOND EPISTLE OF ST. PETER THE APOSTLE.

In this epistle St. Peter says, (chap. iii.) :—" Behold this second epistle I write to you ;" and before (chap. i. 14) :—" Being assured that the laying away of this my tabernacle is at hand." This shows, that it was written a very short time before his martyrdom, which was about 35 years after our Lord's ascension. In this epistle, which has been doubted by some ancient writers, he admonishes the faithful to be mindful of the great gifts they received from God, and to join all other virtues with their faith. He warns them against *false teachers*, by describing their practices and foretelling their punishments. He describes the dissolution of this world by fire, and the day of judgment.

In harmony with the foreknowledge of his own dissolution, and that of his description of the dissolution of the world, St. Peter leaves us in this epistle a true pastoral letter, his last will and testament as it were, his most important legacy, in order to prevent us from falling away from the true faith, to prevent our losing any of the spiritual riches which he had bequeathed to the everlasting flock of Christ, and to preserve us from the forfeiture of our eternal salvation. What, in writing his first epistle, he may have imagined to happen, he now practically and prophetically knew ; he saw what had, and beheld what was come to pass, namely : that men would throw off the authority of the Church, and, full of presumption and self-sufficiency, seek their salvation in *their own*

OPINION, in *their own construction* of the sense of the histories, gospels, and epistles of the sacred writers, not to speak of their corruption of the sacred text itself.

This last, and most of all, important legacy of the Prince of the Apostles, addressed by him to the Christians of the whole world, has, alas! in proportion to its importance, been also more scandalously, and from its very clearness, more *culpably* neglected and trodden underfoot by Protestants, than any other apostolic writing. Mark it well, my dear reader: after you have got the legacies of gospels and epistles from other apostles and *their disciples*, you here befittingly, almost last of all, receive the most important one of all, from that *one* apostle, who was to *confirm his brethren* (St. Luke xxii. 32), who was to feed the lambs and the sheep, the laity and the clergy of the Church of Christ; he therein does not only give you advice, how these sacred legacies may conduce to your salvation, but warns you also, points it out to you, how they will *inevitably lead to your destruction*. Hear then again from the head of the apostles, what has been told you already at page 11 :—" Understanding this FIRST, that no prophecy of Scripture is of any *private interpretation*. For prophecy *came not by the will of man at any time:* but the holy men of God spoke, inspired by the Holy Ghost."—(i. 20, 21.) (True religion, you see, cannot come from reason.) " As also in all his (St. Paul's) epistles, speaking in them of those things; in which are certain things *hard to be understood*, which the *unlearned and unstable wrest*, as they do also the *other Scriptures*, to their own destruction." (iii. 16.)

This, we should hope, would finish the Scriptures *as a rule of faith*, with every *thinking* man.

23.—THE FIRST EPISTLE OF ST. JOHN THE APOSTLE.

The same vein of divine love and charity towards our neighbour, which runs throughout the gospel written by the beloved disciple and Evangelist St. John, is found also in his epistles. He confirms the two principal mysteries of our faith : the mystery of the Trinity, and the mystery of the incarnation of Jesus Christ the Son of God. The sublimity and excellence of the evangelical doctrine he declares :— " And this commandment we have from God, that he, who loveth God, love also his brother," (iv. 21), and again :—" For this is the charity of God, that we keep his commandments ; and his commandments are not heavy." (v. 3.) He shows how to distinguish the children of God from those of the devil : marks out those who should be called antichrists : describes the turpitude and gravity of sin. Finally he shows how the sinner may hope for pardon. It was written, according to Baronius's account, 60 years after our Lord's ascension.

St. John tells us plainly enough in his first and second chapter, why he writes this epistle ; to speak of it as a rule of faith, after what he himself says of it, would be folly. He speaks however of THE true rule of faith, saying (iv. 6) :—" We are of God. He that knoweth God, *heareth* us," (the pastors of the Catholic Church.) " He that is not of us, *heareth us not. By this* we know the spirit of truth, and the *spirit of error."* What a simple, what a beautiful test, to be made use of by those, who sincerely seek their salvation ! How soon will this test discover to them the *true* and the *false teacher, the spirit of truth,* and the *spirit of error !*

24.—THE SECOND EPISTLE OF ST. JOHN THE APOSTLE.

The apostle commends Electa and her family for their steadfastness in the true faith, and exhorts them to persevere, lest they lose the reward of their labour. He exhorts them to love one another, but with *heretics to have no society, even not to salute them.*

Although this epistle is written to a particular person, yet its instructions may serve as a lesson to others, especially to those, who from their connexions, situation, or condition in life, are in danger of perversion. It is as far from being "a rule of faith," as it is positive in the condemnation (*without any qualification,*) of those, who revolt, and do not continue in the *doctrine delivered,* to which *none but the Catholic Church* have ever adhered.

This, as well as his third epistle, was doubted by some ancient writers.

25.—THE THIRD EPISTLE OF ST. JOHN THE APOSTLE.

St. John praises Gaius for his walking in truth, and for his charity: complains of the bad conduct of Diotrephes, and gives a good testimony to Demetrius. Pride, revolt against St. John even, against authority, against the true rule of faith, caused this short epistle to be written.

26.—THE CATHOLIC EPISTLE OF ST. JUDE THE APOSTLE.

St. Jude, who wrote this epistle, was one of the twelve apostles, and brother to St. James the Less. The time it was written is uncertain, only it may be inferred from verse 17, that few or none of the apostles were then living, except St. John. He inveighs against the heresies and wicked practices of the Simonians, Nicolaites and Gnostics, &c., describing them and their leaders by strong epithets and similes. He exhorts the faithful to contend earnestly for the faith *first delivered to them* (what faith was first delivered to this country?) and to beware of heretics. The object of his epistle—anything but a rule, or part of a rule of faith—is obvious to the most ordinary understanding; the true faith had been delivered to the children of the Church, by *word of mouth*, as it was, and is still done to all nations ; and he warns the faithful against all those, who, like ancient and modern heretics, "*separate themselves from the Church of Christ, which is his undivided body ; sensual men, having not the spirit.*" (v. 19.)

Did you never *examine*, my dear reader, whether there are really any heretics and false teachers, and who they are? Or did the apostles, in speaking of them, warn of wolves that existed only in their imagination? Do you know historically of men, that *separated themselves* from the great and undivided body of the Church? Or did the Church separate from Luther and his kindred? What a simple test for finding out a heretic, so simple and yet so neglected:—"beware of men who separate themselves."

This epistle was doubted by some ancient writers, and therefore also called in question by Luther, against whom it so effectively tells. Grotius fancies it to have been written by Jude, the fifteenth bishop of Jerusalem, in the reign of Adrian. The tradition of the 'Church maks its divine authority and original unquestionable.

27.—THE APOCALYPSE OF ST. JOHN THE APOSTLE.

In the first, second, and third chapters of this book are contained instructions and admonitions, which St. John was commanded to write to the Seven Bishops (not to the laity) of the Churches in Asia. And in the following chapters, to the end, are contained prophesies of things that are to come to pass in the Church of Christ, particularly towards the end of the world, in the time of Antichrist. It was written in Greek, in the Island of Patmos, where St. John was in banishment by order of the cruel Emperor Domitian, about 64 years after our Lord's ascension, and was also doubted by ancient writers.

As this Revelation of St. John is literally a prophecy, which according to St. Peter, is *not of any private interpretation*, no one will pretend its being a rule of faith, though many, unfortunately, *wrest* this very part of the gospel, more than any other, to *their own destruction and damnation;* sensual men, revolting in their spiritual pride, against the Church, and against the explicit interdict of the Prince of the Apostles. Apostates, self-justifiers, heretics and hypocritical reformers, seducers and seduced, who, (according to the words of the saintly Anna Catherina Emmerich) in their sickly imagination, haughty imposture, and fanatical excitement, mock and persecute her; and according to their lusts, in the interpretation of their conceit, tear and divide the seamless garment of their Saviour's Church, each one wishing to have her different from what, out of love He made and gave her. Numbers, who with proudly shrugging shoulders, and with shaking head, pass by her, who extends to them her saving arms, towards the abyss that awaits them. Numbers again, that do not dare publicly to deny her, but with effeminate loathing, like the Levite before the poor that had fallen among robbers, pass by before the wounds which they have helped to make in the Church of Christ. Others, that forsake His wounded bride, as cowardly, unfaithful children do their mother at night, when robbers and murderers break in, to whom their dissolute life has opened the door. Others again, who follow the stolen booty, the golden vessels and the broken necklace, that are carried away into the desert. Men that separate from the true vine, to encamp under the wild one; who like erring sheep, exposed to wolves, and driven about by hirelings on barren pasture, will not enter into the fold of the Good Shepherd, who gave His life for His sheep. Men, who wander about without a home, and will not see His city on the mountain that cannot be hidden; who, without unity, are tossed to and fro by changing winds on the sand-waves of the desert, but will not see the house of His bride, His Church, built upon the rock, with whom He has promised to be unto the end of the world, and against whom the gates of hell were not to prevail. Men, that will not enter through the narrow gate, that they may not bend their necks ; who follow those that entered elsewhere but at the right door ; who build mutable, variegated huts on the sand, without altar and without sacrifice, with vanes on the roofs ; and according to these their doctrine varies. Men that contradict each other, and do not understand, that there is no resting place for them : often breaking down their cabins, and hurling their ruins against the corner-stone of the Church that stands unmoved. Men, in whose house darkness is reigning ; yet they will not go to the light that is put on the candlestick in the house of the bride, but with closed eyes they wander without the enclosed garden of the Church, on whose fragrance alone they still live ; they stretch out their arms after dissolving views, and follow wills-o'-the-wisp that lead them to wells without water; on the brink of the pit they will not hear the voice of the calling bride, and hungry, with proud pity, they smile at the servants and messengers who invite them to the marriage feast. They will not enter the garden, for they are afraid of the thorns of the hedge ; intoxicated with themselves they famish without wheat, and perish from thirst without wine ; and blinded by their own light, they call the Church of the incarnate Word, invisible ; men, who will not carry the cross after Him, will not follow Him in His bride, in His city built upon the mountain. But you, my dear reader, if you are not yet in this visible city, in this type of the heavenly Jerusalem, then take to heart the words of the Alpha and Omega (Apoc. xxii. 14) : " Blessed are they that wash their robes in the blood of the Lamb : (not in imagination, but in reality by the sacrament of penance in the Church of the living God), that they may have a right to the tree of life, and may enter in by the gates into the city." If you do this, if you follow no longer those that have changed, added to, and taken away from, the word of God, so fearfully denounced by the Holy Ghost (Apoc. xxii. 18, 19) : then you will find it easy, with the grace of God for which you have to beseech Him, to ascend the steep mountain of the Lord, until you arrive in the holy city, at the seat of St. Peter, and finally in the New Jerusalem of eternity.

A FEW WORDS ON THE CHIEF AIM OF THE GOSPELS AND EPISTLES.

Having cursorily examined each particular book of the New Testament, the truth of the reasons previously given for their ever having been written, will not less clearly have been perceived by the candid reader, than the absence therein of all and every vestige, of the Bible being a rule of faith, or its having ever been intended as such, whether the sacred writings be taken individually or collectively, will have forced itself upon his mind. He will moreover have noticed, that, excepting the gospels as simply historical accounts of our Saviour, all the epistles of the apostles have but one prominent and chief aim, namely :—to *inculcate obedience to those who have the rule over the Church of Christ*, and to warn the faithful *against false teachers*, pointing out at the same time, in the most simple manner, how these wolves in sheeps' clothing infallibly may be known, in order to shun them. St. John, the loving and beloved apostle, admonishes the faithful, "to avoid those *that separate themselves.*" Now from the beginning there was the community of the apostles, of their successors, and the flocks committed to their care, all one united body, forming that visible "Church, to which were added daily such as should be saved." (Acts ii. 47.) It was thus easy to see, who separated from this visible communion. The Church grew up, and we continue to see, how in every age, one heretic after the other, often with multitudes in his train, separated from this one and undivided fold. The Church, though dispersed throughout the world, was visible enough in the assemblies, in the councils of her pastors; and the voice of these councils, of the good shepherds of the fold of Christ, also loudly enough pointed out and proclaimed, "those *who separated themselves*, sensual men, having not the spirit." (Jude i. 18.) Thus, no one ever could, or ever can plead ignorance, down to this very day, in following to destruction *any one who separated himself*. Though not one only, but legions even were to fall away, they would still be those *who separated themselves*. In this, the Church of Christ is not unlike the kingdoms of the earth; hers is indeed a by far more extensive empire, than even that of the greatest nation; her provinces are by far more numerous; and her authority, being divine, is far superior in essence and in fact, than any, which armies and navies, wealth and earthly power can confer.

Now in the one, so in the other it is very easy to see who *separates himself*, who *separate themselves*. Do individuals, families, provinces, colonies, by quitting or rebelling against the empire of this country, *separate themselves*, or does the empire separate from these? Does the deserter separate from the regiment, or does the regiment separate from the deserter? Did the heretics and schismatics, did the Catholic province of England separate from the Empire of the Church? Or did the Church separate from these? The answer is very easy; but, to make the separation of the so-called Reformers, and of several Catholic provinces of the Church, more marked, more manifest, tangible even to the meanest capacity, the providence of God had decreed: that at that time, of the misnamed Reformation, there should be universal peace; that the empire and authority of the Church should be undisputed, unquestioned; that she should be seen by all nations as the real city on the mountain, the Church on the

Rock, with the quiet ocean of the world beneath her sceptre of charity; that the powers of hell, overcome, and tired as it were, of their continual warfare against the Church, over which they are not to prevail, should lie prostrate; that in this universal calm it might be the more easy, for a child even, to know and avoid those, who would arise to make dissensions, or would *separate themselves, sensual men*, having not the Spirit of Christ and His Church.

In this universal repose of Christendom it was, that seemingly prostrate in the conflict with the spouse of Christ, hell was preparing her most desperate onslaught, was transforming the fallen priests of the Church of God into seeming apostles of Christ. (2 Cor. xi. 13.) Luther arose, and soon after him followed a host of "false apostles and deceitful workmen;"—"*some* shall depart from the faith, giving heed to spirits of error, and doctrines of devils;" (1 Tim. iv. 1, also 2 Peter iii. 3, Jude i. 18), and these "some" were not only manifest to all the world, but Luther himself proclaimed it, saying: "at first I stood alone:" thus forcing upon every hearer the knowledge of his apostacy from and rebellion against the Church. But he, who with his fellow Reformers, was to have been avoided as *separating himself*, and, according to the warning of the apostle, shunned like a pestilence; was, alas! followed by numbers who, like himself, could no longer bear the yoke of Christ; was in particular followed by those, kings and princes, who from the beginning were always the last to embrace, and the first to forsake the religion of Christ; and thus, the whirlwind raised by the powers of darkness gathered strength, and in its destructive course devastated some of the fairest fields of the Church. There you behold the manifest, the violent separation from the Church, from the body of Christ, the inundation as it were, of a part of the Catholic globe. But as weeds last only a certain number of years, so here also; the black seed of dissension, the cockle of the enemy, the weed which the whirlwind, which the flood carried in its train and deposited in its own congenial soil, has now well nigh reached its height; and withering away upon the exhausted mud of corruption, let us hope, that it will conduce again to fertilise the land which it covered, making the soil ready for the reception of the good seed of that ever faithful husbandman, the Catholic Church. O, my dear reader! do you still want to know *who they are that separate themselves?*

Trusting, that with the help of God, we have satisfactorily shown to you *from Scripture itself*, that the sacred writings are no rule of faith, that you should avoid all dissenters and separatists, but *obey* the lawful authority of the Church: we will now briefly give you

PROOF FROM REASON, THAT THE BIBLE *cannot* BE A RULE OF FAITH,

always remembering, that religion does not come from reason, not from the *will of any man*, but must of necessity come from manifest divine revelation or authoritative teaching.

The child does not speak, you *teach* it to speak; it has no ideas, it does not understand, but you *teach* it to have ideas, *teach* it to understand; it does not understand what *it reads*, you *teach* it to do so. In this manner you speak to the child of religion, and you *make it understand;* it thus understands *as you do*, because you have taught it so to understand. If you place four different versions of the Bible before the child, point out to it that, which you *think* the correct, the true one: it then learns from your *verbal teaching, by tradition*, that the Bible is the word of God, and that such or such a translation is the true, and the others the corrupted gospel of Christ. It thus believes of christianity, of the Bible, exactly what you believe, through your *verbal* traditionary teaching; its knowledge does not proceed *from reason.* Do you believe however, that, though teaching, you yourself understand *correctly?* Are you *infallible* in construing, in understanding rightly? If you think so: where did you get your *certain* knowledge? Call back to your mind the years of your childhood; how did *you* learn? how did *you* learn to understand? Was it from *verbal teaching?* Were your teachers *infallibly right* in what they taught you in religion? Or, did you forsake their teaching, when you came to *think for yourself;* and did you then put *your own* construction upon what you read? Were you *manifestly inspired* in construing what you were reading? Or did you construe, did you understand *from reason?* If so: is your reason infallible? If not, as you must confess it to be: can you put faith in a book, in which to believe you have *no other ground* save the *fallible guidance* of your own reason, or of *fallible human authority,* telling you, PRE- VIOUSLY *even to your opening the Bible,* that therein you are to read, therein to seek your salvation? Can a book save you, of which you know nothing except from human tradition; a book too, which with all your traditional knowledge of it, you are *not infallible in understanding rightly?* Would it not be preposterous, if a medical work, though plain in its English, were put into the hands of every patient, and the doctors sent to the whereabouts? Would it not be still more preposterous, nay, exceedingly laughable if it were not too serious, to see any man or woman, learned or illiterate, attempting his or her own cure from a book, of whose contents they could not have the slightest notion, unless it were from *previous teaching,* and from competent teachers too? And is it not the same with the Holy Gospel, which in the hands of the doctors of the Church, or under their teaching, is the remedial book of the soul? Can you, my dear reader, with any claim to common sense, still cling to the Bible as your only means of salvation, when, without *previous traditionary teaching*, you can have BUT AN OPINION on the book, just as you might reasonably have an OPINION on a medical work without being previously taught? Where is the *certain* KNOWLEDGE to save you, to come from?

If then, without *previous teaching* there can but be opinion: can you blame your child, if grown up, it forsakes your *opinion* on religion and the Bible, forsakes your *uninspired teaching* for what its *own reason* may suggest? For with our reason,

"With our judgment, 'tis as with our watches,
None go just alike, yet each believes his own."—*Pope.*

And so we must do also in matters of religion, if we have not the Catholic Church, the Church of God to guide us. Hence the Protestant is bound to respect the sincere convictions of every one, though near and dear and differing from himself, and you cannot chide your child for departing from your teaching; for, just as little as you can proclaim yourself infallible, just as little can you, without committing a grievous sin, coerce the conscientious conviction of your child, force your *fallible opinion*, your *uncertain* teaching upon any person, not even on your offspring; can you expect and exact obedience in matters of religion.—Just as little as you know to read, much less to understand *any book* without previous teaching; just as little as you understand even what with your own eyes *you see* (much less when described only) of the commonest trades, of arts and science, of mechanism however simple, without previous verbal teaching; just as little as without previous *infallible* teaching, your vaunted reason can tell you which is the fly and which is the elephant, nay, even who are your own father and mother; just as little as you can distinguish the spurious bank note from the good one, without previous teaching; just as little as from two or three sovereigns, much less from twenty, of various and deteriorating alloy, you can distinguish and pick out the pure one without previous teaching: just as little do you know *any thing certain* and *least of all*, the *true sense*, of the Bible, without previous infallible teaching; it would be folly for you to pretend it.

Thus we know absolutely nothing, not even how to eat and to drink like civilized beings, except *by being taught*. Knowledge, derived from teaching, and appertaining to the things of the world, we may from our own reason further develop, we may improve upon; it may direct us to *things* previously unknown; but religion, coming from God only, and being perfect even as God is perfect, we can neither invent, nor discover, nor improve; we can have no knowledge of it, unless it *be taught us*, either by direct and manifest revelation, or by the teaching of an infallible, divinely instituted authority; we may, like all those who from the beginning left the Catholic Church, wander away from this teaching, we may try to improve upon it, we may even invent a religion: but then our religion ceases to be divine, and ceases to be true; it becomes a human religion, made by man, if not suggested by the devil, and consequently *cannot save us*. Therefore, no one out of the pale of the Catholic Church, can be saved in *virtue of his religion,* though it is to be hoped, that invincible, innocent ignorance of the *true faith,* which our Saviour came to bring us *for our salvation,* will plead in favour of multitudes of our fellow-christians, to whom no opportunity was ever given of learning the true faith, and be a passport to them into everlasting bliss.

True religion, the sun of the soul, is like the sun of heaven; the doctrines, the sacraments, the means of grace of the one, the rays of both, are independent of the will and reasoning faculties of man; both do and must come from without, the human heart must open itself to receive them in the way God pleases; you may shut out each, you may break the rays of each, but nothing from within can ever supply their place ; no religion emanating from the brain, no fire kindled by the hand of man will do.

As God sends forth the rays of the sun, *always the same and everywhere alike*, to gladden the whole creation, so in mercy does He send forth the rays of His divine religion, through pastors by *Himself* appointed, to gladden the heart of man. Through these faithful pastors, who are the instruments of the Holy Ghost, the same as heretics are the tools of the devil, He imparts, *always the same and everywhere alike*, the holy doctrines and graces of His heavenly religion, to whoever is prepared to receive them. These divine doctrines, including the sacraments, the means of grace of the Church, too sacred to be violated, too holy to be defiled and corrupted, God knew better how to preserve pure and how to diffuse, when He chose the apostles, and a successive uninterrupted priesthood for this purpose ; He knew better—*though Protestants give Him no credit for it*—than to write and print them into books, and scatter them all over the globe without faithful and infallible teachers ; He knew better than to allow antiquarians, writers, transcribers, translators, printers, and in particular, wicked falsificators, to provide for the unadulterated preservation and transmission of His Gospel, and to substitute their frail machinery for that which He created and commanded ; He knew better than to exalt a piece of stone, a piece of wood, or some printed sheets of paper, into the dispenser, into a judge of His divine religion ; He knew better, though Protestants give our Saviour no credit for it, than to establish WITHOUT PROVIDING A REMEDY, a rule of faith liable to be corrupted, a rule moreover, which for 1500 years, few, save priests and princes could possess ; a rule which *at this hour millions cannot obtain, and millions cannot read*. If you will escape the guilt of libel against the wisdom of our Saviour, if you will not incur the penalty of a practical denial of his divinity ; then you must concede, that He could not establish a dead book to propagate His merciful dispensations, that He could not leave to mankind the legacy of His divine doctrines and sacraments, without appointing *a succession of lawful executors*, to watch over their due and unadulterated, over their pure and infallible preservation, administration and propagation. No master of the house would leave his family for any time, and leave written instructions behind him for the government of his household, without appointing some *living authority* to supply his place in his absence; and do you really think, dear Protestant reader, that Christ could leave His family on earth, and act less naturally, less wisely, than His creature?—that He would constitute *anarchy* the normal state of His Church and kingdom on earth?

Thus we have seen, that, whatever it may be, but particularly in matters of religion, we know absolutely nothing, unless *previously taught* by some *competent* authority; as also, that it would be inconsistent with the wisdom of Christ, if He had left us no such *competent authority*, infallibly to teach, explain and propagate the written and the unwritten word of God; and this authority which He actually left us, is no other than the Catholic Church.

However, apart from all this, we have above all, still to examine:

I. How we are sure, whether the Bible is actually the word of God.
II. Whence and how this sacred book has come down to us.
III. What actually constitutes the "Canon," or the "inspired books" of the Scriptures.
IV. Whether these books have been kept pure and uncorrupted.
V. Whether and how their true sense and meaning has been preserved.
VI. Whether, and when the Bible has superseded the authority and verbal teaching of the Catholic Church.

c

We will now proceed to explain these points in as brief a manner as possible, fondly hoping, that their exposition will induce you, for ever to lay aside the Bible as your *rule of faith*, and cast your anchor in the Church of Christ.

I.—HOW ARE WE SURE, WHETHER THE BIBLE IS ACTUALLY THE WORD OF GOD.

That the Bible is the word of God, is taken for granted by every denomination of Christians; it is taken for granted on *general tradition*, for the Bible itself bears no witness of itself *in any way;* nor do Protestants ever examine or consider, whether it is rightly transmitted, rightly translated, rightly printed, rightly read, and *rightly understood;* but, as said before, all is taken for granted, it is taken on *general tradition*.

Christ did not testify of Himself, but God testified of Him by the miracles which He performed, by His spotless life, by His wisdom, that He was the Son of God, that He spoke and taught the word of God.

The apostles did not testify of themselves, but their testimony was Christ, their evidence was God in the working of miracles.

Timothy, Titus, and the other immediate successors of the apostles did not testify of themselves as true teachers of the word of God, but God testified of them, partly by the miracles which they performed, and partly by the apostles, the witnesses of their divine ministry, and by whom they had been ordained and appointed to *teach* the gospel. In the epistles of St. Paul we have seen, how he gave testimony to the above bishops, as well as to Onesimus, Tychicus, Epaphroditus, &c., as true teachers of the word; the apostle was their witness, as Peter, James, John and Barnabas (Acts ix. 26, 27 : Gal. ii. 9,) had been witnesses of himself.

The pastors of the Catholic Church are not their

own witnesses; but the authority of the bishops of the Church is the testimony of their divine mission; from predecessor to predecessor, up to Titus, Timothy, Onesimus, St. Paul, all the other apostles, and Christ Himself, who moreover, through the power of the Holy Ghost, has given additional testimony of the Church, by all His promises, and by the many miracles that in every century have been wrought by her sainted children.

Heretics arose; they had *neither the Holy Ghost*, nor any *preceding authority* to testify of them, and yet many unfortunately believed them.

Lastly, a sacred book, accidently, ignorantly, and intentionally corrupted (speaking of course of the Protestant Bible), a dead object, that cannot see, hear, or speak, is sold in a shop, and upon the authority of the bookseller, or upon general belief *previously taught* by the so-called Reformers, is taken to be the *word of God* without any further inquiry. The book itself does not anywhere refer to any preceding, living or dead authority; does not say whether it is correct or not, whether it is a completion or but part of a whole, or whether it is the word of God, of man, or of the devil; but notwithstanding all this, it is not only, without the slightest scruple, taken as the word of God; but even as such, exclusive of everything else; and thousands of deluded persons moreover stake their salvation upon the unassisted reading of it, without any further teaching, explaining it as well as they can by the light (?) of their own reason.

Taking for granted however, that the Bible is correctly transmitted, translated, printed, &c., it nevertheless does not follow, that it is the word of God; because, firstly, it is not, and cannot be, a witness of itself; secondly, because there is not one syllable of its being the word of God in the Bible itself; thirdly, because it cannot be tried by its own internal evidence, for it can give no evidence of itself; the evidence must be exterior and infallible.

Thus, the only claim in favour of the Bible as the word of God, rests entirely upon tradition ; tradition Protestants reject, and yet upon tradition they recêive the Bible, upon tradition they receive moreover the corrupted word of God as pure!

That the Bible can be no witness of itself, must be clear to the most moderate understanding, when not only the apostles and their successors, but even Christ Himself, were or could not be witnesses of themselves or of their teaching, as we have amply seen at page 64.

That there is not one syllable in the sacred Scriptures, saying, that each book individually, or all collectively, are the word of God, every Bible-reader must acknowledge.

That to human reason, *even with previous teaching*, the Bible presents no feature of its being the word of God, is no less evident, than that it can give no testimony of itself. If it possessed that internal evidence of being the word of God, it would not be rejected by so many nominal Christians as well as by Jews (as far as the New Testament is concerned), Turks, heathens, &c. Protestant Christians generally take it to possess this evidence, because they are inclined to this belief from *previous teaching*. The same reasons of internal evidence, which Christians bring in favour of the Bible as the word of God, are brought by Turks in favour of the Koran, by the Hindoos in favour of the Vedas, and by all, with the like sincerity of belief. This shows of itself, that human reason, unenlightened by authoritative teaching, can have no conception of what is the word of God and what is not ; and that without this divinely-instituted authoritative teaching it would be in vain, if even the Bible possessed that internal evidence of being the word of God, which Protestants ascribe to it. Witness this humiliating fact in the preaching and teaching of the various sects ; each *hearer* believes his preacher to deliver the word of God, whether it be for Christ or against him, for baptism or against it, for certain doctrines or against them. Thus, human reason and the Bible, both mislead us, and it is well that Christ should have left us a living authority in the Catholic Church, the divine enlightener of the one and the infallible and true interpreter of the other. That the Bible contains sublime narratives, mysteries, and prophecies, is no evidence whatever of its being the word of God ; for there are other works, of the same contents, and, perhaps more elegantly, more captivatingly expressed; there are books of prophecies, which may be called prophecies of the devil ; there was the girl at Ephesus who prophecied, and yet she had a devil.

It must then strike every one, that the Bible being the word of God, rests on no other foundation whatever, except tradition. This tradition we have first from our parents, and from our spiritual teachers; these again had it from their forefathers and predecessors. Then again, one party had it from Wesley, another from the Established Church, another from Calvin, another from Luther, &c.; and Catholics have it from their Church. The former, having separated from the Universal Church, had naturally no tradition, save that which they derived from her teaching ; and thus we find *all tradition* concentrated in this Church, up to the apostles themselves, who formed and called her Catholic. She preserved and propagated, from her we have learned, the knowledge of her own origin and foundation ; it is her who tells us, that certain of her apostles and their immediate successors, St. Luke and St. Mark, wrote what we call, the New Testament. From her however we not only learn, that these holy men simply wrote what constitutes this sacred volume, which, if not guided by some power above, and higher than their reason, will and memory, would make it but the writings of some holy men, the mere words of men ; but we learn also from her exclusively, that what they wrote was under the inspiration of the Holy Ghost ; and *this alone* could make it the word of God. They have not, however, attested that fact in writing, either in their gospels, or epistles, or anywhere else, but must have communicated it to those of *the faithful* who were about them ; that fact must have been preserved by tradition, as well as that SS. Mathew, Mark, Luke, &c., were actually the writers of their respective gospels and epistles. The apostles and their successors, though inspired by the Holy Ghost *to teach* and *preach* the gospel, were not necessarily, or as a matter of course, inspired in what *they wrote;* all they wrote, though true, was not on that account written by inspiration : for St. Barnabas, who received the Holy Ghost, wrote also, yet his epistle is not considered to be inspired, and therefore not included in the canon of the Scriptures. There is no doubt, that many of the immediate successors of the apostles, like SS. Mark and Luke, wrote likewise ; but why should the writings of the latter be considered as inspired, when those of the former, like that of St. Barnabas, and the epistles of St. Clement, of which we shall have to speak hereafter, were not so considered ? For this reason only : that these had been handed down by the undisputed tradition of the Church as inspired, whilst the others had not this evidence in their favour.

Another kind of external evidence may be brought as a proof of the inspiration of the holy Scriptures, namely ; the fulfilment of their prophecies. But unfortunately for Protestants, their Protestantism gives the lie to the sacred word of God in this most important point, as, besides other instances, it has no sacrifice, no pure offering, no incense to offer to the Lord of Hosts (Malach. i. 11) ; nay, not in any place, much less "from the rising of the sun even to the going down of the same." Thus, if any form of Protestantism were true, it would necessarily prove the holy Scriptures to be false ; but Protestants acknowledging the Scriptures to be inspired, it proves their religion to be false.

Again does Protestantism give the lie to the sacred

word of God, in as much as there is no generation of Protestants in whom the prophecy of Mary, the Mother of God (St. Luke i. 48), has been fulfilled. Oh! if this were so, the Blessed Virgin, through whom Christ gave himself to us, and through whom He in return bestows all His graces upon those who praise and honour her, Protestantism would not exist. It is not too late for *you of good will*, to rank yourself among the children of Mary, to become a brother of her firstborn child Jesus, in that Church of which she is the Mother, and to find therein that peace, which angels from heaven proclaimed for those alone of *good will*, at the birth of your Saviour. Come then, be not ashamed or afraid to follow the Holy Ghost, to say with the archangel and with us : " Hail, Mary, full of grace, the Lord is with thee : blessed art thou among women." (St. Luke i. 28.) Follow the inspiration of St. Elizabeth, and repeat again and again : " Blessed art thou among women, and blessed is the fruit of thy womb." (St. Luke i. 42.) Then, as she received her Lord only through the Blessed Virgin, so you will only receive Him through her ; at her voice of salutation, her voice of intercession, your soul will leap for joy, like the infant in the womb of St. Elizabeth (St. Luke i. 43, 44), and with this holy woman you will exclaim : " Whence is this to me, that the Mother of my Lord, the Mother of my God, the Mother of God, should still think of me, should come to me, should bring my Saviour to me ?" Do this, and in you also will be fulfilled the prophecy of Mary, the Mother of our Lord : " From henceforth all generations shall call me blessed." But as Protestantism never called, never calls her blessed, it must therefore be false, or the Bible uninspired. In the Catholic Church however, the prophecies of the Holy Ghost have been literally fulfilled; and thus we have it only from *her* internal and external evidence, that what we consider the Bible, but more particularly the books of the New Testament, have been written by the holy men whose names they bear; from *her* alone we know for certain, that the writers were inspired by the Holy Ghost in these their writings; from *her* alone,, from *her* verbal teaching, from *her* scrupulously preserved tradition, "*holding firmly even the form of sound words*" (2 Tim. ii. 13, 14), we know infallibly, that the Bible is the word of God, *when correctly transmitted, translated, and printed,* and above all, *correctly explained;* without these essentials it is the word of man, and when wilfully perverted and corrupted, it becomes the word of Satan.

Now if the Catholic Church be, or ever has been, fallible or corrupt in her tradition, you must not take the Bible from her hands at all; if on the other hand she be infallible and pure in her tradition, you must not only take the book, but also its text and interpretation, as handed down at the same time by her uninterrupted, unaltered and unalterable teaching.

Having shown you, that but through the Catholic Church alone we are sure of the Bible being the word of God, we will now trace the

II.—PROGRESS OF THIS SACRED BOOK FROM THE APOSTLES' DOWN TO OUR PRESENT TIME.

Before we examine, whence and how the Holy Scriptures have come down to us, we will just say a few words on the ancient manner of writing, then give a short account of the descent of the Old Testament until its attachment to the New, both together forming what is called the Bible, or the Book of Books.

The most ancient manner of writing was a kind of engraving, whereby the letters were formed in tablets of lead, wood, wax, or similar materials; this was done by styles made of iron, brass or bone. Instead of such tablets, leaves of papyrus, a weed which grew on the banks of the Nile, (also of the Ganges), were used first in Egypt; afterwards parchment, made of fine skins of beasts, was invented at Pergamus, In the eighth century, paper was made of cotton and silk, and in the thirteenth century of linen ; of quills, the earliest mention appears in the seventh century. Books anciently writ only on one side, were done up in rolls, and when opened or unfolded, filled a whole room ; but when written on both sides on square leaves, were reduced to narrow bounds.

From this it will be seen, that of old, the difficulties of writing, translating, reading, and the preservation of writings, were infinitely greater than at present, and that consequently forgery, and the corruption of the Scriptures, like every other writing, was in proportion more easy and likely to happen, both from wicked intent, as well as from every other cause which operates in our day, to forge, corrupt, and adulterate wills, letters, and other literary productions. As to intentional falsifications, no book was ever more exposed to them, than the sacred Scriptures on the part of heretics, as may easily be imagined, particularly on looking to the later wilful corruptions of Luther and other so-called Reformers. In treating of the transmission of the Bible, these considerations ought constantly to be borne in mind.

The Greek translation of the Old Testament, commonly called of the 70, or by its Latin name Septuaginta, was made by the Jews living at Alexandria, and used by all the Hellenist Jews. This version of the Pentateuch, or the five books of Moses, appeared about 285 years before Christ, the remaining books somewhat later, and at different times. The Jews even of Palestine at first gloried in the translation, but it being employed by the Christians against them, they began soon after the beginning of the second century, to condemn it, alleging that it was not always conformable to the Hebrew original. This text had then suffered several alterations by the blunders, and according to Kennicott, some few by the wilful malice of transcribers ; though these differences are chiefly ascribed by Origin to alterations of the Hebrew text, introduced after the version was made. William Carpenter (Protestant) says on this head : " that the Hebrew moreover, had become completely a dead language, not only to the Hellenists, but to the Jews generally, that they could obtain no knowledge of their Scriptures(but through the medium of a translation ;" and therefore, the Septuagint having been exploded and expelled from every Synagogue, in order to supply its place, three new versions were set on foot amongst them. The first was formed in 129, by *Aquila*, of Sinope, in Pontus, whom the emperor Adrian, when he built Jerusalem, under the name of Aelia, appointed overseer of that undertaking. He had been baptized, but for his conduct being expelled from amongst the Christians, became a Jew, and gave his new translation out of hatred to the Christians. A second was published about the year 175, by *Theodotion*, a native of Ephesus, some time a Christian, but a disciple first of the heretic Tatian, then of Marcion. At length he fell into Judaism, or at least connected obedience to the Ritual Law of Moses with a certain belief in Christ. His translation, which made its appearance in the reign of Commodus, was bolder than that of Aquila. The third version was framed about the year 200, by *Symmachus*, who having first been a Samaritan, afterward, upon some disgust, turned Jew. In this translation he had a double view of thwarting both the Jews and the Christians. St. Jerome extols the elegance of his style, but says he walked in the steps of Theodotion ; with the two former translators, he substituted νεανις (young female or woman) for παρθενος (virgin) in the famous prophecy of Isaias (vii. 14), and in that of Jacob, (Gen. xlix. 10), τὰ ἀποκειμενα αυτω' for ω ἀποκειται. Both which falsifications St. Justin Martyr charges upon Aquila, and St. Irenæus reproaches Aquila and Theodotion with the former.

Many additions from these versions, and several

various readings daily creeping into the copies of the Seventy, which were transcribed, to apply a remedy to this danger, Origen compiled his Hexapla. He was a native of Alexandria, a scholar of St. Clement, then regent of the famous catechetical school in that city, and from his unwearied assiduity in writing, surnamed Adamantius, which is "Diamond." Possessing every thing necessary to qualify him for his arduous undertaking, he published the aforesaid work in 231. It contained the Holy Scriptures in Hebrew, the same in Greek letters: the Greek versions of Aquila, Symmachus, the Seventy, and Theodotion, in six columns corresponding to each other. In his Octapla he added two other Greek versions, viz.: a fifth, found at Jericho, and a sixth at Nicopolis in Epirus. In his Eneapla, according to W. Carpenter, he added a seventh copy; containing the said *fifth, sixth,* and *seventh* copies, so called because their respective authors or editors are unknown, and the six versions of the Hexapla. Origen's Tetrakla consisted only of the versions of Aquila, Symmachus, the Seventy, and Theodotion. So many expositions had crept into the common copies of the Seventy, or Septuagint, with infinite variety amongst themselves, that this performance of Origen was of great advantage. To every word in the margin, which was an explication or an addition, borrowed from any of the other three Greek versions, allowed by the Jews, he prefixed an asterisk, or star (*). To all such words as were not found in the Hebrew as then extant, he prefixed an obelus, or dagger (†). The signification of two other marks, which he had made use of, is not very well known: the one called lemniscus, a kind of double obelus (‡); the other hypolemniscus (※). The asterisk is much the most frequent mark, and an omission of it before any word by the carelessness of a copyist, was sufficient to introduce a foreign word into the text. Respecting the text itself, W. Carpenter says:—"that he left it untouched; and only pointed out, by certain marks, the difference between that (the Septuagint) and the Hebrew text with which he had collated it," thus preserving it quite pure. The original work of Origen, which was deposited by him with his other writings in the library of Cæsarea, is supposed to have perished when that city was taken and destroyed by the Saracens in 653, after a siege of seven years.

Before the year 300 three other corrected editions of the old Greek version were published, the first by *Lucian*, the second by *Hesychius*, and the third by *Pamphilus*,* the martyr. The first was made use of in the churches, from Constantinople to Antioch; that of Hesychius was received at Alexandria, and in the rest of Egypt; and the third in the intermediate country of Palestine, as we are informed by St. Jerome. The edition of Lucian came nearest to the common edition of the Seventy, and was the purest. The excellent Vatican MS. (called Codex Vaticanus from being kept at the Vatican at Rome) of the Seventy, published (though with some amendments from other MSS.) by Cardinal Carafa, at the command of Sixtus V. in 1587, is said in the preface to have been written before the year 390. It is proved from St. Jerome's letter to Sunia and Tretela, and several instances, that this Vatican MS. comes nearest to the Seventy, and to Lucian's edition. It originally

---

* This Saint who had established a public school of sacred literature at Cæsarea in Palestine, distributed many copies of his versions gratis, for he was of all men the most communicative and beneficent, especially in encouraging sacred learning. He employed almost his whole life in writing and adorning the books of the Holy Scriptures. Mauntfaucon (Biblioth Coislin. c. 20) gives an account of a copy of the epistles of St. Paul, written in the 5th or 6th century, (kept among the Greek MSS. af the Coislinian Library, comprised in that of the Abbey St. Germain-des-Prez at Paris) collated with a copy of St. Paul's epistles in the handwriting of St. Pamphilus, kept in the 5th age in the library of Cæsarea.

contained the entire Bible, according to W. Carpenter, but is now imperfect in both Testaments. The old Alexandrian MS. known under the name of *Codex Alexandrinus*, presented by Cyrillas Lucaris, patriarch of Constantinople, who obtained it at Alexandria, to King James I., and kept in the British Museum in London, is thought by one to have been written about the year 396, by others, about one hundred years later. It was published by Grabe, though not pure; for in some places he gives the reading of this MS. in the margin, and prefers some other in the text. Though none of Origen's asterisks are retained, it comes nearest to the edition in the Hexapla; in some places it is conformable to Theodotion, or Symmachus, and seems mostly the Hesychian edition; it was also published by Patrick Young the keeper of the king's library, at Oxford in 1633.

Thus we see about the year 400 a variety of Greek Old Testaments, one differing from another, with the Hebrew notoriously corrupted or lost, when St. Jerome appeared, and out of this mass of perplexities, of this chaos of differences, formed one clear stream of light, one undeceptive oracle of the Church.

Before entering upon the whole Bible, let us first trace the progress of the gospels and epistles of the New Law, until in St. Jerome we unite both the Old and the New Testament in one work, as the record of God's mercies to mankind, but not as their rule of faith; for it is evident from what has been said, even if every individual Christian had known to read, and perfectly understood Greek and Hebrew, that the Old Testament could not have been a guide, much less an exclusive one, to salvation.

THE NEW TESTAMENT.

In treating of the New Testament, we have seen already under the head of each gospel and epistle, why, when, and in what language they were written, though upon either of these points there exist a variety of opinions among the learned, alone more than sufficient, for ever to discard the idea of their being, or their having been intended, singly or collectively, as a rule of faith. There is no record of what has become of the originals, save that doubtful one of St. Mark's gospel; but we know, through and from the universally concurring testimony of the Church, that in the lifetime of the apostles and their immediate successors, they were translated into the then living languages, though isolated (the gospels and epistles) from each other, according to their being scattered in the various parts of the Church. By degrees, through the communion of all the Churches, they being all as one body in faith and doctrine, forming but One, Holy, Catholic, and Apostolic Church, the various copies and translations—for, the originals were no doubt jealously guarded by those to whom they were addressed—were exchanged among them, and in proportion to this exchange, became collected, until we see the earliest of these translated collections in the Peschito or literal Syriac version, which, according to Carpenter, is ascertained upon undoubted evidence, to have been made, at the latest, towards the close of the second century, and is attributed, upon grounds of very high probability, to the close of the first or to the earlier part of the second century. In the same manner we see, according to the same authority, the old Italic* or ancient Latin version, which, as he says, was certainly made before the end of the second century, as it was then quoted by Tertullian: it was universally read throughout Europe and Africa, as the former was throughout the East.

* Dom : Martianay published, in 1695, the ancient Italic version of St. Matthew's gospel. Since that time an old manuscript copy of the four gospels in the true ancient Italic version, was found at Corbie, and published at Verona.

The Italic contained also a Latin translation of the Old Testament, *made from the Greek in the time of the apostles*, and probably approved or recommended by some of them, especially according to Ruffinus* (the friend and contemporary of St. Jerome), by St. Peter, who, as he says, sat twenty-five years at Rome. That it was the work of several hands is proved by Dr. Milles, who, during the space of thirty years, examined all the editions and versions of the sacred text with indefatigable application,† by Calmet,‡ and by Blanchini.§ In the fourth century great variations had crept into the copies, as St. Jerome mentions, so that almost every one differed, For, many that understood Greek, undertook to translate anew some part, or to make some alterations from the original. However, as Blanchini observes, these alterations seem to have been all grafted upon, or inserted in the first translation : for they seem all to have gone under the name of the Latin Vulgate, or common translation. Amongst all these copies, the before-mentioned Italic, most likely so-called, because it was chiefly used in Italy and Rome, was by far preferable to all the other Latin editions, as St. Austin testifies. Up then, to the time of St. Austin, no one will pretend the possibility of the Bible, in any version, whether Hebrew, Greek, Syriac or Latin, to have been a rule of faith, much less the exclusive one ; for it was the Church only, the concurrent testimony of her pastors, that was able to decide on the correctness or impurity of this or the other version or copy, and in the same manner to pronounce unerringly on the true meaning of the text ; because in either case the Church declares *facts* as they were delivered to her, and no *opinions*.

Thus, as with the Greek Old Testament about the same period, we see a vast variety of Latin versions and copies of the Bible, of equal diversity and per-

---

* Invect 2.   † Miles in Prolegon.   ‡ Disser : sur la Vulgate.
§ Praef : in Evan. Quadruplex.

plexities, from which nothing could extricate, but a Church, who was in possession of all the facts connected with everything relating to the written word of God. And the Church to do this, existed then as it continues to exist unto this day; nothing was more wished for by her, whose common traditional consent had already from the beginning pointed out the Italic as the best of the Latin versions, than to see an end put to the many corruptions of the written word of God, which in all ages she has been so anxious to preserve as pure as the doctrines it contains.

As God in His mercy always raised up men in His holy Catholic Church, fit to cope with difficulties and dangers that beset her course, so here also, to remedy so serious an evil as that spoken of, He provided His spouse with a St. Jerome, in every way capable of undertaking and accomplishing so arduous a task. The Church acknowledges him to have been raised by God through a special providence for this purpose, and particularly assisted from above; and she styles him the greatest of all her doctors in expounding the divine oracles. Pope Clement VIII. scruples not to call him a man, in translating the holy Scriptures, divinely assisted and inspired. He was furnished with the greatest helps for such an undertaking, living many years upon the spot, whilst the remains of ancient places, names, customs, which were still recent, and other circumstances, set before his eyes a clearer representation of many things recorded in Holy Writ, than it is possible to have at a great distance of place and time. The Greek and Chaldaic, as well as the Latin, were then living languages, and the Hebrew, though it had ceased to be such from the time of the captivity, was not less perfectly understood, (as we have seen, page 71, by the translation of Aquila, &c.), and spoken among the doctors of the law in its full extent, and with the true pronunciation. It was carefully cultivated in the Jewish Academy or great school of Tiberias, out of which St. Jerome had a master. It has long since become very imperfect, reduced to a very small number of radical words, and is only to be learned from the Hebrew Bible, the only ancient book in the world extant in that language. Most of the rabbinical writers are more likely to mislead us in the study of the Hebrew sacred text, than to direct us in it; so that we have now no means to come at many succours which St. Jerome had for his task. Among others, the Hexapla of Origen, which he possessed pure and entire, were not the least: and by comparing his version with the present remains of those of Aquila, Theodotion and Symmachus, we find he had often recourse to them, especially to that of Symmachus.*

Above other conditions, it is necessary that an interpreter of the holy Scriptures be a man of prayer and sincere piety. This alone—not dry learning—can obtain light and succour from heaven, give to the mind a turn and temper which are necessary for being admitted into the sanctuary of the divine oracles, and present the key.

Our holy doctor was prepared by a great purity of heart, and a life spent in penance and holy contemplation, before he was called by God to this important undertaking. Through His servant Pope Damasus, to remedy the inconvenience of such a variety of editions, and to correct the faults of bold or careless copiers, he was commissioned first, to revise and correct the Latin version of the gospels by the original Greek: which the saint executed to the great satisfaction of the whole Church. He afterwards did the same with the rest of the New Testament. This work of St. Jerome's differs very much in the words from the ancient Italic, of parts of which some copies are extant. It insensibly took its place in all the Western Churches, and is the Latin Vulgate of the New Testament, which is now everywhere in use. The edition

* See Calmet Disser: sur la Vulgate.

of the Greek Septuagint which was inserted in Origen's Hexapla, being the most exact extant, St. Jerome corrected by it the ancient Italic of many books of the Old Testament, and twice the Psalter: first, by order of Pope Damasus at Rome, about the year 382; and a second time, at Bethlehem, about the year 389.

His new translation of the books of the Old Testament, written in Hebrew, made from that original text, was a more noble and a more difficult undertaking. Many motives concurred to engage him in this work, as: the earnest entreaties of many devout and illustrious friends, the preference of the original to any version how venerable soever, and the necessity of answering the Jews, who, as we have seen before, in all disputations would allow no other. He did not translate the books in order, but began by the books of Kings, and took the rest in hand at different times. This translation of St. Jerome's was received in many Churches in the time of St. Gregory the Great, who gave it the preference. And in a short time after, St. Isidore of Seville wrote that all Churches made use of it. They retained the ancient Italic version of the Psalter, which they were accustomed to sing in the divine office; but admitted by degrees, in some places the first, in others the second correction of St. Jerome upon the Septuagint; and this is printed in the Vulgate Bible, not his translation. The old Italic without his correction is still sung in the church of the Vatican, and in St. Mark's at Venice. The books of Wisdom and Ecclesiasticus, the two books of the Maccabees; the prophecy of Baruch, the books of Jeremias, the additions at the end of Easter, and the thirteenth and fourteenth chapters of Daniel, and the Canticle of the Three Children, are in the ancient Vulgate, because they were not translated by St. Jerome, not being extant in Hebrew or Chaldaic. The remainder of the Old Testament in the present Vulgate is taken from the translation of St. Jerome, except certain passages retained from the old Vulgate or Italic.

Thus we see completed the most perfect work of the Scriptures that ever existed, that everywhere received the sanction of the Church, and which since then, at all times, and in all places, has been regarded by her as the standard work of the written word of God. How well it deserves the high esteem in which it has been held since its production, needs, after what has been said, no further demonstration. Up to the so-called Reformation, there was no dissentient voice respecting its unrivalled excellence, which, having been acknowledged all over the Church of Christ for more than 1100 years, received again the final seal of authority, by the concurrent testimony of the whole Catholic Church, represented in the assembly of her pastors, congregated from all nations, at the Council of Trent. By this voice of the Church, on the 27th of May 1546, it was declared as an authentic version of the Bible, and recommended to be preferably used by her pastors and children; but it was not meant by this decree, that any preference should be given to it above the pure original text.

The Catholic Church no more denies that immaterial faults may, and did creep into the Latin Vulgate, that it is declared by her to be an infallible rule of faith; and a great many verbal differences and lesser faults having crept into several copies, through the mistake of printers, and before printing, through transcribers, the Church used the greatest industry imaginable to amend and rectify them, as you may read in the preface to the Sixtine edition. Pope Pius IV. caused not only the original languages, but other copies to be carefully examined. Pius V. prosecuted that laborious work; and by Sixtus V. it was finished, and by him commanded to be put to press in 1585, from whence it issued in 1590, the last year of his pontificate. Yet notwithstanding the bull prefixed before his Bible, then printed, the same Pope Sixtus, as is seen in the preface made 1592, after diligent examination, found that no few faults slipped

into his impression, by the negligence of the printers:
and therefore, he both judged and decreed, to have
the whole work examined and reprinted; but that
second correction being prevented by his death, was
after the very short reign of three other popes,
undertaken, and happily finished by his successor
Clement VIII., answerable to the desire and absolute
intention of his predecessor, Sixtus: whence it is,
that the Vulgate, now extant, is called the correction
of Sixtus, because this vigilant Pope, notwithstanding
the endeavours of his two predecessors, is said to
have began it, which was according to his desire,
recognised and perfected by Clement VIII., and therefore
is not undeservedly called also the Clementine
Bible: so that Pope Sixtus's Bible, after Clement's
recognition, is now read in the Church, as authentic,
true Scripture, and is the very best corrected copy of
the Latin Vulgate.

The zeal thus shown for the purity of the word of
God on the part of the Catholic Church, is unquestionable,
and must be evident to her bitterest enemy;
and in proportion to this zeal has she ever been ready
to condemn the corruptions which at various times
took place, and by which the faithful were sought—
alas! not unsuccessfully!—to be deceived.

From this standard work of the Latin Bible, though
not exclusively, translations into the living languages
were made by the sons of the Church at all times,
particularly by, and under the direction of the monks,
to whom we owe almost entirely the preservation of
the written word of God, and whose labours (as we
shall see hereafter) sufficiently show, how intent the
clergy were of multiplying and disseminating the
sacred writings. We have seen this already in the
early Syriac and Latin versions of the Church, these
languages being then the *languages of the people;*
and the latter continued to be very commonly understood
in Europe, but particularly by those who could

read and possess books, until some time after the so-called Reformation.

According to Bagster, the Latin versions were used among the Saxons after their conversion, A.D, 596.— About the time of Constantine the Great, when Christianity found entrance into Ethiopia, the whole Bible was translated into Ethiopic. Towards the end of the fourth century, the Bible was translated by Bishop Ulphilas into Gothic; at the beginning of the fifth century it was translated into Armenian; somewhat later into Georgian; in the ninth century into the Slavish, which instances may be seen in the German Protestant Conversation Lexicon of Brockhaus.

At the beginning of the same century, a version into the Teutonic, the German language of his own age, was made by order of Charlemagne; and a rhythmical paraphrase of the gospels, under the direction of the emperor Luis I. As the dialect continued to advance, new versions were executed from time to time; and in the numerous manuscripts of the Bible, or portions of it, with which the libraries of Germany abound, may be traced almost a consecutive history of her language. A distinct German translation, the first *printed* version, the author of which is unknown, was published in 1466; and two copies of this edition are still preserved in the Senatorial library at Leipzig.

From the appendix of Horne to the 2nd volume of his "Introduction to the study of the Scriptures" we learn by a passage which he quotes from Hallam, "that in the eleventh, or twelfth century, we find translations of Psalms, Job, Kings, and the Maccabees, into French." That however not only these books were among the people, but the whole Bible, clearly appears from a decree of the Diocesan, or Provincial, Council of Toulouse in 1229, by which the laity of that district were prohibited from *possessing the Scriptures*, without (as usual in such local and special prohibitions, though rare) the sanction of the pastors; owing to the monstrous errors of the

Albigenses which infected that portion of the Church, and when, in the words of Horne, "after the diffusion of heretical principles, it became expedient to screen the orthodox faith from *lawless interpretation*," interdicted already by St. Peter. However, as said before: there can be no doubt, that the Scriptures were among the people, read, and by the teaching of the Church, understood by them. In No. 2 of the "Dublin Review" for 1836, more details are given; amongst these there is mentioned a catalogue of the library collected by Charles V. of France, written in the year 1373, which contains a notice of a volume comprising the books of Proverbs, Psalms, Wisdom, Ecclesiastes, Ecclesiasticus, Isaias, and eighteen chapters of Jeremias. According to Horne, "Jean de Vignay, or de Vignes, translated the epistles and gospels contained in the Roman Missal in the early part of the fourteenth century; later in the same century, Raoul de Presles, or de Praelles, translated the Bible into French, as far as the Psalms or Proverbs. A very fine MS. of his version is preserved in the Brit: Museum." Subsequent translations will be noticed among the printed versions.

An Italian version was completed as early as 1290 by the Dominican, Jacob à Voragine, Archbishop of Genoa, according to the testimony of Sixtus Senensis.

According to Mariana, the great Spanish historian, the Bible was translated into Castilian by order of Alphonso the Wise; it was translated into the Valencian dialect of the Spanish in the year 1405 by Boniface Ferrier, brother of St. Vincent Ferrier; the epistles and gosples were translated into Spanish, by Ambrosio de Montesma, in 1512.

Into Flemish, the whole Bible was translated by Jacobus Merland, before 1210, as the Protestant historian Usher admits.

In the fourteenth century the Bible was translated into Sweedish, by the direction of St. Bridget.

According to the testimony of the astronomer,

Jonas Arnagrimus, a disciple of the distinguished Tycho Brahe, a translation of the Bible was made in Iceland as early as 1279.

A translation of the Scriptures into Polish was made by order of St. Hedwige, wife of the famous Jagellon, Duke of Lithuania, who, upon his marriage with her, was chosen king under the name of Ladislaus the Fourth. During the same reign, (the close of the fourteenth century) there seems to have been a second version, by And. Jassowitz.

In England, according to Merryweather's "Bibliomania," about 100 years after its conversion by St. Augustin and his companions, Caedmon, the old Saxon herdsman, seems to have been the first to paraphrase the Scriptures into the vernacular tongue, in which he was *joyfully assisted by the monks* of Whitby, though but a herdsman. At page 127 our author says of him, "that he was not only the father of Saxon poetry," but to him also belongs the inestimable honour of being the first who attempted to render into the vulgar tongue the beauties and mysteries of the holy Scriptures; his paraphrase is the first translation of the holy writ on record. So let it not be forgotten that to this Milton of old (encouraged by the Church) our Saxon ancestors were indebted for this invaluable treasure. He was wont—the author says at page 125—to make "pious and religious verses, so that whatever was *interpreted to him* out of Scripture, he soon after put the same into poetical expressions of much sweetness and humility in English, which was his native language. By his verses the minds of many were often excited to despise the world and to aspire to heaven. *Others after him* attempted in the English nation to compose religious poems, but none could ever compare with him, for he did not learn the art of poetry from man but from God."*

* Bede, 6, iv. c. 24.

"He was indeed, as the Venerable Bede says, a poet of nature's own teaching: originally a rustic herdsman, the sublime gift was bestowed upon him by inspiration, or as it is recorded, in a dream. As he slept, an unknown being appeared, and commanded him to sing. Caedmon hesitated to make the attempt, but the apparition retorted," "Nevertheless, thou shalt sing—sing the origin of things." Astonished and perplexed, our poet found himself instantaneously in possession of the pleasing art; and, when he awoke, his vision and the words of his song were so impressed upon his memory, that he easily repeated them to his wondering companions.* He hastened at daybreak to relate these marvels and to display his new-found talents to the monks of Whitby, by whom he was *joyfully received*, and as they unfolded the divine mysteries, "the good man," says Bede, "listened like a clean animal ruminating; and his song and his verse were so winsome to hear, that *his teachers wrote them down*, and learned from his mouth."†

Next to the paraphrase of Caedmon, among the cherished labours of the Catholic Church in England we first find the work of Adhelm, first Bishop of Salisbury, who, according to Horne, translated the Psalter into Saxon, in the year 706; and at his earnest persuasion also, Egbert, or Eadfried, Bishop of Lindisferne, or, Holy Island, soon after executed a Saxon version of the four gospels. Not many years after this, according to the same authority, the learned and Venerable Bede, who died in 735, translated the entire Bible into that language.

We then have the Saxon translation of the New Testament of King Alfred, which was printed at London in 1571, and more correctly at Dort, with

---

* John de Trevisa, says: "Caedmon of Whitaby, was inspired of the Holy Ghost, and made wonder poisyes an english, meiz of al the Storyes of Holy Writ."—MS. Harleian, 1900, fol: 43, a. † Ibid.

notes, in 1664. A beautiful MS. copy, which belonged to Archbishop Tiegmund, is preserved in the Cottonian library. This illustrious king, according to Horne, undertook also a translation of the book of Psalms, but died A.D. 900, when it was about half finished.

The Protestant Bagster gives the following account of the early English versions, in his English Hexapla.

The gospel of St. John was translated by Bede in the eighth century, and appears to be the first portion of the New Testament translated into the Anglo-Saxon, the vernacular tongue.

A manuscript of the four gospels of St. Jerome's Latin version was copied by Eadfried, afterwards Bishop of Lindisfarne (whose *translation* of the four gospels we have noticed above), in the year 680; this manuscript was greatly adorned by Ethelwold, his successor in his see (with the assistance of Bilfrid, his anchorite,) with golden bosses and precious stones as well as very curious illuminations. To this manuscript, an interlined Anglo-Saxon version was, at some subsequent period, *added by a priest* named Aldred; the date of this version is much questioned, but the reign of Alfred appears to be regarded as about the most probable period. This manuscript is known by the name of the *Durham Book*.

There is another Anglo-Saxon version of the four gospels, probably of the same antiquity as the one just mentioned. This version, like the former, is interlined, the Anglo-Saxon word being placed over the corresponding Latin. This valuable and interesting manuscript is in the Bodleian Library, and from the name of a former owner, is called the *Rushworth* gloss.

In the tenth century a partial gloss of the books of Proverbs was executed, the version being inserted between the lines of a Latin copy, through a considerable part of the book.

In the latter part of the same century were executed the version and paraphrases of Aelfric of the historical books of the Old Testament. He wrote, also, a summary account of the Old and New Testament, from which we learn what the portions of Scripture were which he turned into Anglo-Saxon. The following appears the result of his labours: the Pentateuch, Joshua, Judges, part of the history of the Kings as found in the six books, Samuel, Kings, and Chronicles; Easter, Job (perhaps) Judith and the two books of Maccabees. Part of this version was printed in 1698.

There exists a third Anglo-Saxon version of the four evangelists, which appears to have been made at a later period than the other two. The translator is unknown, but he appears, in several places at least, to have translated from the Latin version which was in use before the time of Jerome, if, indeed, he has not wholly followed such a copy. This version has been several times printed, first of all in 1571. This edition was not very accurate, but other editors have bestowed care in amending the text, Junius collating for this purpose *four manuscripts of this version*, as well as the translations in the Durham Book and the Rushworth Gloss.

Besides this translation of the gospels, a few manuscripts containing the Psalter are mentioned as having been written shortly before the time of the conquest. A little later than this there appears to have been an Anglo-Norman version of the gospels into the dialect which was now displacing the genuine Anglo-Saxon; there are three such manuscripts known to be in existence, one of which is attributed to the time of William the Conqueror, the other two to about the time of Henry II. These three manuscripts all exhibit the same translations, although with variations made by the copyists; it is probable that each one sought to frame the language of the version according to what was most intelligible to himself.

After this summary of the Anglo-Saxon translations and paraphrases, Bagster continues:

Some time after the Norman conquest had supplanted the Anglo-Saxon language by the then created English, no distinct versions of the Scriptures or parts thereof seem to have been made, but several paraphrases and versions in metre. The following is a summary of what were the translations and paraphrases into English subsequent to the Norman conquest and previous to the latter part of the fourteenth century:

The paraphrase in metre, without rhyme, of the Gospels and the Acts of the Apostles, executed by Ormin, therefore called "Ormulum."

The metrical paraphrase of the Old and New Testaments, contained in the collection entitled "Sowlehele" (no doubt from the German "Seelenheil," salvation of the soul) supposed to be prior to the year 1300.

The Northern paraphrase of Genesis and Exodus (of about the same date) in Corpus Christi College, Cambridge.

The metrical Psalter, of about the same date.

The revised version of the Psalms, somewhat more modern than the preceding.

The prose version of the Psalter, by Richard Rolle of Hampole before the middle of the fourteenth century.—Brit: Museum.

The metrical version of the Penitential Psalms, part of Job, and the Lord's prayer by the same.

Two other prose versions of the Psalms.

The gospels of Mark and Luke, and the epistles of St. Paul.—Benet College Cambr.

The Northern translations of the Gospels for the Sundays throughout the year.—MS. Brit: Mus.

According to Horne, the first English translation of the Bible, known to be extant, was executed by an unknown individual, and is placed, by Archbishop Usher, to the year 1290. Of this, there are three MS. copies preserved; in the Bodleian library, and in the libraries of Christ Church, and Queen's Colleges at Oxford.

Then we have still the translation into the English

language of the whole Bible, made in the fourteenth century by John de Trevisa, vicar of Berkeley, in the county of Gloucester; Horne attempts to throw some discredit on it, and Bagster omits it entirely, but it is admitted by Wharton, Usher, and Antony Wood.

Extensive as, according to this Protestant authority, the labours of the Church (of which a more particular account in the second number of the "Dublin Review," 1836), must have been, considering the many copies that unquestionably were made of the versions enumerated, but lost through wars and the destructive character of the so-called Reformation:* they must

---

* Bale, the Protestant Bishop of Ossory says on this subject:—Never had we been offended for the loss of our libraries, being so many in number, and in so desolate places, for the more part, if the chief monuments and most notable works of our most excellent writers had been reserved. If there had been in every shire of England but one solemn library to the preservation of those most noble works, and preferment of good learning in our posterity, it had been somewhat. But to destroy all without consideration, *is, and will, unto England, be for ever, a most horrible infamy,* among the grave seniors of other nations. A great number of them which purchased these superstitious mansions, reserved those library books, some to serve their jakes, some to scour their candlesticks, and to rub their boots. Some they sold to the grocers and soapsellers, and some they sent over sea to the bookbinders; not in small numbers, but at times *whole ships full,* to the wondering of foreign nations. Yea, the Universities of this realm are not all clear in this detestable fact. But cursed is that belly which seeketh to be fed with such ungodly gains, and so deeply shameth his natural country. I know a merchantman, which shall at this time be nameless, that bought the contents of two noble libraries for forty shillings price: a shame it is to be spoken. This stuff hath he occupied instead of grey paper for the space of more than these ten years, and yet he hath store enough for as many years to come. A prodigious example this, and to be abhorred of all men, which love their nation as they should do. Yea,

have been immensely greater still than here appears,
as in all ages she kept thousands of men, having no
other employment than that of transcribing the holy
word of God, which she had commanded to be studied
in every religious house, in every university, in every
ecclesiastical college, and expounded to the faithful
in every place and at all times. The "Bibliomania"
of the Protestant F. Somner Merryweather, though
based on the scanty remains and catalogues of ancient
Catholic literary achievements, gives a beautiful picture of the industry of the monks, their vast labours
in the preservation and diffusion of ancient writings,
and of the Scriptures in particular. With what fondness and admiration does he not speak of the monks
of Glastonbury, and of the beautiful library they had
accumulated; and yet with what a deplorable preju-

what may bring our realm to more shame and rebuke, than
to have it noised abroad that we are despisers of learning?
I judge this to be true, and utter it with heaviness, that
neither the *Britons*, under the *Romans* and *Saxons*, nor yet
the *English* people, under the *Danes* and *Normans*, had
ever such damage of their learned monuments, as we have
seen in our time. *Our posterity may well curse this wicked
fact of our age, this unreasonable spoil of England's most
noble antiquities.*" (John Bale, Declaration in Leland's
Journal, An. 1549. Fuller, Ch. H., B. VI. p. 335.) D'Israeli,
after giving a summary of this extract from Bale, adds, "the
fear of destruction induced many to hide manuscripts under
ground, and in old walls. At the Reformation (?), popular
rage exhausted itself on illuminated books, or MSS. that
had red letters in the title-page; any work that was decorated was sure to be thrown into the flames as superstitious.
Red letters and embelished figures were sure marks of being
papistical and diabolical. We still find such volumes
mutilated of the gilt letters and elegant flourishes, but the
greater number were annihilated. Many have been found
under ground, being forgotten. What escaped the flames
were obliterated by the damp." (Curiosities of Literature,
vol. I. p. 85.)

dice does he lament the destruction of the abbey and its treasures! "Well," he says at page 145, "years rolled on, and this fair sanctuary remained in all its beauty, *encouraging the trembling Christian, and fostering with a mother's care the literature and learning of the time.* Thus it stood till that period, so dark and unpropitious for monkish ascendancy, when Protestant fury ran wild, and destruction thundered upon the heads of those poor old monks! A sad and cruel revenge for *enlightened minds* to wreak on *mistaken piety* and *superstitious zeal.*" And all these extraordinary exertions of *mistaken piety and superstitious zeal*, to multiply and place the Bible in the hands of the faithful, were made, as has been shown on Protestant authority, long before Wickliffe appeared, without taking into consideration the testimony of Sir Thomas More, that "the holy Bible, was, long before his (Wickliffe's) days, by vertuous and well learned men, translated into the English tong, and by good and godly people, with devotion and soberness, well and reverently red." We have even the authority of Cranmer to this effect, that the Bible was translated and read in English, long before the so-called Reformation, and without the least restriction. He says: "It is not much above one hundred years since Scripture hath not been accustomed to *be read in the vulgar tongue* within this realm; and many hundred years before that it was translated and read in the Saxon's tongue............and when this language waxed old, and out of common usage, because folk should not lack the fruit of reading, it was translated again into the newer language, whereof yet also many copies be found." (Strype's Cranmer, app. 242.) The translation of the Scriptures by Wickliffe was made from 1378 to 1381 from the Latin Vulgate, and his version may be seen in the English Hexapla of Bagster. It comes nearer to the Catholic translation than any Protestant, and yet the Church found it necessary to condemn it, ever vigilant to preserve the word of God in that purity in which she had received it.

The same desire of the Spouse of Christ, to propagate the unadulterated word of God in the Scriptures, displayed itself with equal intensity after the art of printing had been discovered.

The first German translation of the Bible was printed at Strasburg in 1466, and according to the Protestant Conv. Lex. of Brockhaus, no less than twelve different editions appeared previous to the translation of Luther, which was begun in 1522.

In Spain, the version of Boniface Ferrier (see page 84) was printed in 1478, and reprinted in 1515, *with the formal consent of the Spanish Inquisition.*

In Italy, the country most peculiarly under the sway of Papal dominion, the Scriptures were translated into Italian, by Malermi, a Camaldolese monk, at Venice, in 1471; and this version was republished *seventeen times before the conclusion of that century.* A second version of parts of the Scriptures, was published in 1472; a third at Rome, 1471; a fourth by Bruccioli, at Venice, in 1532; and a corrected edition, by Marmochino, in 1538, four years after Luther had completed his. And every one of these came out, not only with the approbation of the ordinary authorities, but with that of the Inquisition, which approved of their being published, distributed, and promulgated.

In France a translation was published, in 1478; another by Menoud, in 1484; another, by Guiars des Moulins, in 1487; which may rather be called a history of the Bible; and finally, another by Jacques Le Fevre, in 1512, often reprinted.

In the Belgian or Flemish language, the version of Jacobus Merland (see page 84), was published at Cologne, in 1475; before 1488 it had been published three times, and before 1530 it had altogether passed through *seven* editions. A second version appeared in 1518.

There was also a Bohemian translation published in 1488, *thrice* reprinted before Luther's, not to speak of the Polish and Oriental versions.

As one gigantic effort of the Catholic Church shortly before the misnamed Reformation, the Polyglott Bible* of Cardinal Ximenes must not be left without notice, which we take from the "Biblical Companion" of W. Carpenter. "This great and valuable work," he says, "was begun and carried through the press at the expense of this cardinal, whom it is said to have cost 50,000 ducats. The various texts are thus disposed: the Hebrew, Latin, and Greek, in three distinct columns, and the Chaldee paraphrase, with a Latin interpretation, at the bottom of each page. The margin is filled with the Hebrew and Chaldee radicals. Various disputes have arisen as to the authenticity of the MSS. consulted in forming this edition; it has been asserted that the Hebrew text has suffered from the capriciousness of the editors, and that the Greek text was frequently interpolated according to the Latin Vulgate, which emendations could not be found in Greek MSS. In addition to this charge, may be added, that of altering the Greek according to the Hebrew. But both these accusations have been proved to be groundless by Michaelis and Eichhorn. The learned Caesar de Missy charges the editors with having antedated the New Testament, jealously aspiring to appear as earlier editors of so notable a work than Erasmus, whose edition (the value of which will be seen hereafter) was published in the beginning of 1516.—Mr. de Missy has not, however, supported his assertions with any conclusive arguments; we therefore, incline to

---

* Besides this famous Polyglott Bible, there are three others, of which the two elder ones are also the work of the Catholic Church. That of Antwerp appeared in 1572, that of Paris in 1645, and that of the Protestant Bishop Walton *last of all* in 1655; and he preferred to adopt therein the Catholic Greek Bible of Rome before any other.

think, with Mr. Dibdin, that he was mistaken in his *conjectures*. Cardinal Ximenes, whose favourite object was the completion of this Polyglott, did not live long after it was finished. He died in 1517, leaving behind him an unblemished character and an unspotted reputation. He was one of those great men who appear, as comets, but for a time; and he was one of the very few whose memory has been cherished and revered by all parties and all nations."

The hatred of the fathers and more immediate followers of the so-called Reformation to the *pure* word of God, written in letters of gold and adorned with precious stones, has left us but a faint idea of the actual vastness of the labours of the Catholic Church anterior to the invention of printing, whether we consider the constant production and diffusion of Latin Bibles, or of vernacular versions for the space of 1500 years; but since the invention of printing, according to the "Dublin Review" before mentioned, there issued from her presses no less than at least *seventy* editions in various living languages, from 1462 till 1534, without mentioning the thousands of Latin Bibles that were printed and published since 1455, by Guntenberg and Faust alone.

Having thus seen the immense labours of the Catholic Church until the birth of that disastrous period, called the Reformation, we will now proceed to a short review of Protestant exertions and *merit* in the same sphere, and leave to the good sense of the reader, by looking on this picture and on that, to draw his own conclusion, not only respecting the Catholic Church and Protestantism, the Catholic Bible and the Protestant Bible, but also between their respective rules of faith.

Of the efforts of Wickliffe, the distant precursor of Protestantism, we have spoken already; and the Catholic Church can well afford his being fondly quoted by Bible Christians, who have been kept in ignorance of the numerous versions she caused to be

made and copied both before and after his lame and
defective performance, considered though by Protestants, as if they had known the Latin, from which he
translated, better than the whole English Church,
and as if there had been no other English versions
besides, whilst, as we have seen, translations, as well
as Latin copies, commonly understood, were constantly multiplied and diffused as far as the manner
of transcribing would allow.

The actual Protestant labourers in the field of the
sacred writings, began with Luther and Tyndal, both
renegade monks, and the latter an exile from his
country. Wishing to draw the attention of the reader
more particularly to English versions, we beg to refer
him for the doings of Luther to the before-mentioned
number of the "Dublin Review." Tyndal's version,
according to Bagster, was made in 1522 from the
Greek, from the third edition of Erasmus' Greek Testament, the first edition of which was published in
1516; it was worse by far than that of Wickliffe, as
we shall see by and by, and prohibited by Bishop
Tonstall, who charged him with "having craftily translated the Tew Testament into English, intermeddling
therewith many heretical articles and erroneous opinions, pernicious and offensive, seducing the simple
people." Bagster, from whose English Hexapla the
following is taken, says: "It is true that Tyndal's
first edition bears *very evident marks* of haste. The
distinct charges against the translation are that
"priests," "church," and "charity," are translated
"seniours," "congregation," and "love;" and also,
that *grace* was sometimes rendered by *favour, penance*
by *repentance*, and a *contrite heart* by *troubled heart*.
Such were the trifling (!!) reasons assigned for the
prohibition and burning of the New Testament."
After this enumeration of *some distinct*, and *not trifling*
charges, and after the well-known corrections of
Tyndal's false translation, as has been shown in this
work, Bagster has the impudence to say a little further:

"At all events, before the translation was thus prohibited and the book destroyed as being faulty, the errors or wilful perversions in translation *should have been stated*. It is no doubt quite true that the version upholds what Tonstall and More (Sir Thomas) called heresy; but this simply results from its *not* being a perversion of the original (!!!)." And to say this after the perversions have been corrected!!!

"It was also," Bagster continues, "printed in Holland, and differed widely from the English printed edition, as the Dutch had an Englishman to correct the press. Meanwhile the Dutch printers were multiplying the copies of the English New Testament; in this they seem to have been simply actuated by the love of *gain;* their object having merely been profit (so entirely so that they did not even employ an English press-corrector), of course *accuracy* was little cared for; the demand for the copies appears to have been such as to make them saleable, however carelessly executed." And this, Bagster ascribes to the eagerness of the people to possess "the pure word of God"!! No; many of the nobility, clergy, and people panted to be freed from obedience to the Church, panted to be married, to live more easily, without fasting, and confession, and without the performance of good works. This appetite the Reformers satisfied in themselves, publicly preached its indulgence, and *made the written word of God conform to it;* and *hence* the greediness of so many after the "pure word of God (!!)," that excused and sanctioned their godlessness.

Later, these Dutch printers had the aid of George Joyce, who corrupted the Scriptures, according to the same author, by whom he is upbraided for it, as well as by Tyndal at the time, most likely because Joyce went even too far for *him*. Nevertheless the books must have sold as a rule of faith. Tyndal in 1534 revised his work,—which Bagster, from whom we take this, proclaims above as *not* being a perversion of the original — by *correcting* "seniours" into "elders," &c., &c.

And would you ever dream, my dear reader, of comparing such a work as Tyndal's with the Latin Vulgate or any Catholic translation? Or would you even go so far as to take it as your exclusive rule of faith? A Bible moreover, which not only by Bishop Tonstall, but even by Parliament in 1542, was stigmatized as "crafty, false and untrue?"

The next effort of Protestantism in England was that of Myles Coverdale, likewise a renegade, and exiled priest with Tyndal. "He began (according to Bagster) his translation about 1534 and says, he had five sundry interpreters. Now what can these five have been? (1) The Vulgate; (2) Paguinus' version; (3) Luther's German translation; (4) Leo Judas' German Swiss version, and the (5th), the writer of the Hexapla supposes "Sebastian Munster's folio Hebrew Bible with a *Latin Version;*" but it was most likely Tyndal's translation he meant, which according to William Carpenter, formed part of his work.*

Can the reader for a moment think, that, with such defective and miserable second-hand helps, the Vulgate excepted, this translation of Coverdale's contained the pure word of God? And, as if aware of the impure sources from whence he had imposed the pretended word of God upon the people, he later made another translation, taking, according to Bagster, the *Latin Vulgate* for basis.

After the separation of Henry VIII. from the Universal Church, Bibles were translated and published under *his* vicar-general, the layman Thomas Cromwell, and under the succeeding authorities of the *civilized* Established Church, but also repeatedly prohibited by them to be *read*, though not on account of the corruption of the texts. William Carpenter, after giving an account of these versions, says at page 40 of his Biblical Companion:—"We have now enu-

* Bibl. Comp: page 40.

merated the principle editions of the sacred writings that *preceded* the "authorised" English version now in common use. It must not be supposed, however, that these were so many new and independent translations. They were, in fact, only so many *revisions of Tyndal's and Coverdale's versions*, with occasional insertions of the additions found in the *Latin Vulgate*, or in the Septuagint version. The Geneva Bible, *purports* to be a new translation from the originals; but there can be no doubt that its basis was the previous translation, and that it was only "compared diligently with the Greek," as the editor, in one place, inadvertantly admits."

On King James's accession to the throne of England, a new translation was immediately projected, and finished in the space of three or four years, although it was not published till 1611; and this is the present *authorised* version mentioned above. Quoting the directions given by the king for this new translation, W. C. continues, page 41: "It is evident from the translators' preface to the reader, in which they speak of '*building upon their foundation that went before*,' of endeavouring to make that better which they left so good, (!!) and—more conclusive still—in which they aver: "we never thought from the beginning that we should need to make a new translation, nor yet to make of a bad one a good one..........but to *make a good one better*, or, *out of many good ones (!!)*, one principal good one, not justly to be excepted against: that hath been our endeavour, our mark." How very much these labours like those of St. Jerome!— and of the Catholic Church! The idea! of making one principal good Bible, not justly to be excepted against, *out of many good ones*, which, by the previous expression, *were justly described!*

The reading of Bagster's Hexapla, and of the Biblical Companion of Wm. Carpenter, as also of the Bibliomania of Merryweather, will give to every honest Englishman a due notion of the Bible as a rule of

D

faith, a more minute detail of the various English translations, and of the strange material they were made from; it will show him still more the value of Catholic versions, whether made from the Greek, the Hebrew, or the Latin, and the worthlessness of Protestant ones, which also, though but partially, has been demonstrated already in treating of the individual gospels and epistles of the New Testament.

The continental helps which Coverdale in his wisdom made use of for his first version of the Bible, were made; by Pagninus and Luther from the Hebrew, the former, as well as the latter, excessively faulty; and Luther's acknowledged interpolations, and his shameful ignorance of the Hebrew language, rendering him contemptible to his warmest friends, are well known to the biblical student. Some of his falsifications will be noticed later. Leo Juda translated likewise from the Hebrew, and so did Munster, whose version sticks close to the Jewish paraphrase and Rabbins. These were the *second-hand* materials of a so-called Reformer.

There were other translations made from the Hebrew; but to estimate all out of this language properly, let us turn to Wm. Carpenter, a Protestant authority, whose Biblical Companion, page 12, says: "With regard to the Hebrew Scriptures, comprising the books of the Old Testament, it must in candour be admitted, that our knowledge of the formation of the present text is very *imperfect* and *unsatisfactory*. Dr. Kennicott contends, that almost all the existing MSS. were written between the years 1000 and 1460; whence it has been reasonably inferred, that the older manuscripts were *destroyed*, after having been used by the Jewish literati, in revising the common text." After entering into a description of the care and scrupulosity with which the sacred writings were transcribed and preserved by the Jews, he continues page 13: "But we are not more at a loss to discover the method pursued in the revision of the Hebrew

MSS. by the critics of whom we have just spoken, than we are to ascertain the rules adopted by the early editors of the printed editions. The particular MSS. which they used, the way in which they employed their materials, the degree of authority they yielded to preceding editions, and other matters of a similar description, are *all beyond our power to learn; for on these points, they have maintained a complete silence.* We must therefore be contented with a brief sketch of the principal editions;" and he then cites among others the edition printed at Brescia in 1494, edited by Gerson, son of Rabbi Moses.

A celebrated collation of Hebrew manuscripts by the Protestant Dr. Kennicott, which clearly proves the defective state of the Hebrew text, was begun in the year 1760. He himself collated 250 manuscripts; and under his inspection, and at his expense, Mr. Burns collated about 350, so that the whole number collated on this occasion, was nearly 600. It appears, that *in his opinion*, 51 of the MSS. collated for his edition were from 600 to 800, and that 174 were from 490 to 580 years old. The first volume of the collection was printed in 1776; and the second in 1780, *Four quarto volumes of various* readings have since been published by De Rossi of Parma, from more than 400 MSS., some of which *are said to be* of the seventh and eighth century, as well as from a considerable number of rare and unnoticed editions.

The dispute of the learned respecting the Hebrew text of the Bible is not at an end yet, but more than above need not be said, to show the uncertainty thereof, and of the translations made therefrom. It may nevertheless, be well, to give an instance of this uncertainty of these, so to say, modern old MSS. and the incompetency of mere learning to make out the correct text and right sense of the Scripture; and this we will extract from the "Biblical Companion," page 32, where, speaking of the various causes from which erroneous translations arise, Mr. Carpenter says: "The English Bible, which indicates strongly that the translator has been sadly puzzled to make any thing intelligible of his text, (2 Kings vii. 13), reads thus 'And one of his servants answered, and said, let *some* take, I pray thee, five of the horses that remain, which are left in the city (behold, they *are* as all the multitude of Israel that are left in it; Behold, *I say*, they *are* even as the multitude of the Israelites that are consumed), and let us send and see.' If any one can understand this, it is to be wished that the public may have the benefit of his discovery." (!!) After this, Mr. C. would himself translate it as follows: "Behold, they are as all the multitude of Israel which remain in it; behold, they are as all the multitude of Israel which are consumed."—And now read the same verse in the Catholic Bible (4 Kings vii. 13). "And one of his servants answered: Let us take the five horses that are remaining in the city (because they are no more in the whole multitude of Israel, for the rest are consumed) and let us send and see," compare it with the former and say: whether you do not prefer St. Jerome and the Catholic Church, to a translation which makes nonsense of the word of God; and whether it is not absolutely humiliating for human reason, to take such a work too, upon the authority of one or a few individuals, as an exclusive rule of faith, as a safe guide to heaven!

We have now to show still the value of the printed editions of the Greek Bible, and the translations made therefrom, like that of Tyndal; and for this purpose we likewise quote the following from Wm. Carpenter, who says:

"All these Greek versions (spoken of at pages 73 and 74) were collected by the indefatigable Origen, and placed together with the Septuagint and original Hebrew text, in his famous Polypla: and this, perhaps, is *the last entire copy of them,** for the Talmudists having gradually excluded all Greek versions from the Synagogues, and the Christians universally adhearing to the old translation, the rest were either *totally neglected,* or only such parts of them copied into the margins of Bibles and commentaries, as were deemed the most worthy of attention. Thus it was, that the Septuagint triumphed, at length, over all its rivals, and remained for several ages after the sole Scripture and standard in all the Christian Churches. We are not to imagine, however, that it was *exactly the same* in every Church, or that any Church possessed a copy of it *that was perfectly correct;* much less *that any such copy now exists."* And in speaking of this work of Origen he continues: "the text itself he left untouched; and only pointed out, by certain marks, the differences between that (the Septuagint) and the Hebrew text, with which he had collated it. His admirers and followers, however, did not show the same respect to the old text, but *altered* it according to his suggestions, in the copies which they made; and the loss of the autograph renders it impossible to ascertain the extant to which this was carried. From *this revised* text all our present copies of the Septuagint are derived."

---

* There are now four independent exemplars of the Greek version; that of Alcala or the Complutensian, contained in the Polyglott of Cardinal Ximenes, mentioned page 94; that of Venice or the Aldine; that of Rome; and that of Oxford. The Roman edition, begun in the Pontificate of Gregory XIII., and completed in that of Sixtus V., who also corrected the Latin Vulgate, appeared in the year 1587. It was principally taken from the famous Vatican MS., and where it failed, from others of nearly the same antiquity. By many it is thought to be the *most genuine* copy of the old Greek version that has yet been published. The Protestant Bishop Walton adopted this edition in the London Polyglott, at once the indication of a candid mind, and of THE SUPERIORITY of Catholic Biblical labours.

That in these Greek copies of the Old, as well as
in those of the New Testament, innumerable faults
must have crept in* during a period of from 1000 to
1400 years, may be easily imagined; the more so, as
there was no St. Jerome to revise and to form in
Greek, as he did in Latin, when Greek, Latin, and
Syriac were still *living* languages, the Hebrew still
known in all its purity by the Jewish doctors, and
when original manuscripts in these languages, like
the work of Origen, were before him, one clear and
limpid stream, a Greek Vulgate, from which to drink
from age to age, guarded with the utmost jealousy
by the ever watchful pastors of the Catholic Church,
and by them preserved in its original purity, as was
the Latin.

Though then ever so many copies may be collated,
in order to establish a pure Greek text, yet, how is it
possible, that any work, requiring such laborious and
inexhaustible researches, that translations made from
the production of these labours, upon the authority
alone of *individual learned men*, can be considered by
any person of the least understanding, as a rule of
faith established by the wisdom of our Saviour?

According to Bagster, who himself in his Hexapla
adopts as his standard Bible the Catholic Greek one
of the Catholic Dr. Scholz, there were no Greek MSS.
of the New Testament to be had at the time of
Wickliffe, whom he pronounces as incompetent to
translate them if there had been any; he says "that
it was not until after the taking of Constantinople by
the Turks in 1453, that copies of the Scriptures and
other MSS. in Greek became dispersed by the fugi-

---

* 30,000 various readings were found by Dr. Mills in the
Greek *New* Testament. Even the most valuable Vatican
and Alexandrian MSS. of the Bible abound in faults of
the copiers. Patrick Young (in Latin Patricius Junius)
when keeper of the king's library in London, scrupled not
to erase and alter several words in the Alexandrian Greek
MS. of the Bible, as is visible to this day.

tive Greeks throughout the Western part of Europe, until Dr. Linacre (an eminently learned physician and afterwards priest, about 1500) introduced Greek literature into England, there was scarcely any thing known in this country either of that language or of works therein."

Having seen, how every thing Greek was new in Europe in the latter part of the fifteenth century, and the general state of Greek manuscripts of the Bible, let us now learn from Wm. Carpenter the particular value of the Greek Bible of Erasmus, from whose third edition Tyndal made his English translation. Our author says:

"The first edition of the New (Greek) Testament appeared in the year 1516, under the editorship of the celebrated Erasmus. The MSS. upon which he formed his text, were *only four* in number, and the three of which he is found to have made the greatest use, contained *only parts* of the New Testament, and in other respects were not of very high value. In addition to his MSS., Erasmus consulted the writings of some of the Greek Fathers" (of course of the Catholic Church before the Greek schism) "and also the *Latin Vulgate;* and where, in cases of difficulty, these afforded him no assistance, he corrected" *(the word of God) "from conjecture"*!!! (How different from the labours of Catholic Biblical authors!) "It is plain, therefore, from the character of the materials of which Erasmus was possessed, that however learned and acute he may have been, his edition of the Greek text cannot possess the very highest degree *of excellence.** True it is, that in his subsequent editions he made numerous alterations; but notwithstanding that many of them were real improvements, they do not materially alter the character of his texts."

Such was the foundation of Tyndal's eulogised

* Our Protestant author would have done better to say, that it had no excellence at all; but he looks at it with the eyeglass of sectarianism.

Bible, which again became the basis of succeeding
translations; and these again, with his, and with
such Greek and Hebrew assistances as our Protestant
friend describes, served in turn: "*to make out of
many good ones, one principal good one,*" viz.: the present
authorised version of the Established Church!!

Such then is the source of salvation of those, who
out of the Catholic Church take refuge in the Anglican
lay establishment and other Protestant denominations,
and who, if not there themselves, take their
versions of the written word of God, as an exclusive
rule of faith!

English Catholic labours respecting the Bible, seem
to have been at a very low ebb after the invention
of printing. So many worldly and idle pastors that
were evidently neglecting their flocks and preparing
them as well as themselves for the fall, left to the few
good shepherds no time or thought for Bible printing,
when moreover the number of translations and Latin
copies in the land, in proportion to those who could
read, did not perhaps so urgently require it; and
when, above all, the men of power, wealth, and learning,
instead of sacred, patronised profane literature in
preference, as we see from the list of Caxton's printed
works; there was no inducement for the English
printer, to engage in printing Bibles for a nation, the
flower of which, for the greatest part, was rotten and
dead already to the maxims and precepts of the
Catholic gospel, until the separation of the good from
the bad took place. Then, as we have seen, *those
who separated, sensual men, having not the spirit,*
(Jude i. 18), made Bibles to suit their new and easy
faith, whilst the good, those who at home escaped the
block or gallows, in foreign countries found asylums,
where, as usual, founding colleges and seminaries,
they issued their first English printed New Testament
at Rheims in 1582; translated by William, afterwards
Cardinal Allen, Gregory Martin, and Richard Bristow,
all of the Rhemish college. It was reprinted at

Antwerp, in the year 1600; and the whole Bible was published, after the college was restored at Douay, in 1609, 1610. It was afterwards revised by the Rt. Rev. Dr. Challoner. In the year 1750, an edition, in which the phraseology was modernised, the notes abridged, and in some instances considerably altered, was published in London, under his inspection. This is the Douay Bible now current among the Catholics of these countries. It has been printed very frequently, not only at home, but also in New York, Philadelphia, and many others of the States of North America.

It has not been our object to speak at length of the labours of the Catholic Church, contemporary with the mock reformers, or after the mock reformation, as it would beyond necessity extend these pages; however, the Polyglottes mentioned page 94, the Latin Vulgate as revised by the Popes named page 81, the Greek version of Pope Gregory XIII., see page 103, the Greek Bible of Dr. Scholz, are already palpable evidences of the superiority of her performances, whether in Hebrew, Greek, Samaritan, Latin, or living languages; but for a better view of Catholic productions in general, during and after the sad transformation of religion, see the "Dublin Review" mentioned before.

Thus the history of the transmission of the Bible from the time of the apostles to our own, seems on all hands, even on the part of Protestants, to exalt the Latin Vulgate,* the standard Bible of the Catholic Church.

---

* The value of this version has already been shown by the recourse to it of almost every Protestant translator of the Bible; and it is more enhanced still by the direct testimony of Protestant Biblical critics. Thus the distinguished George Campbell says: "The Vulgate may be pronounced on the whole a good and faithful version." In "Horne's Introduction," the author says of this version: "It is allowed

Having seen how the Bible was transmitted to us, let us now briefly examine what actually constitutes

III.—THE CANON OF THE HOLY SCRIPTURES,

or in other words, those books which the Church receives as inspired by the Holy Ghost, and how this Canon of the Scriptures was established. It will be made evident, that this knowledge cannot be derived without the Catholic Church, which is; the Supremacy of the Roman See, in communion with all the Churches; in fact, through that which in the Apostle's Creed we profess to believe, viz.: "the communion of the saints" on earth. That this communion existed in the first ages, as it exists to this day in the Catholic Church between the Churches of all countries and nations, is amply proved by Protestant authority—if proof there need be—in as much as they rest the chief testimony in favour of the sacred writings, upon this very communion of the Churches, and the concurrent testimony of their pastors.

That a communion of churches, like other bodies, civil or political, must have some common centre of attraction and a binding or uniting power, an axle round which harmoniously to move, cannot only not be denied, but is proved by every social institution, from each individual family to the most extensive empire. That this centre of the Christian Church was at Rome as it is this day, we have partly seen already in the existence of Pope Damasus and his governing the Church, and in his instructions to St. Jerome to revise and correct the text of the Holy Scriptures.

to be in general a faithful translation, and sometimes exhibits the sense of Scripture with greater accuracy than the more modern versions," (and very naturally so) . . . "The Latin Vulgate preserves many true readings, where the modern Hebrew copies are corrupted."

But one of the earliest visible instances perhaps, of the supremacy of the Roman Church, not unlike, as it were, to the hardly visible leaf of a seed just emerged from the ground, we find in an epistle written by Pope Clement, who followed St. Peter, St. Linus, St. Cletus, in the apostolical chair in the year 91, to the Corinthians, (among whom there existed an impious and detestable division, as the saint called it) which on account of its excellency and esteem, in which it was held in the primitive Church, was placed in rank next to the canonical books of the Holy Scripture, and with them read in the Churches, whence then also it was found in the Codex Alexandrinus, mentioned page 75, in the British Museum. We have a large fragment of a second epistle of St. Clement to the Corinthians, found in the same MS. of the Bible: from which circumstance it appears to have been also read like the former, in many Churches, which St. Dionysius of Corinth expressly testifies of that Church, though it was not so celebrated among the ancients as the other. John James Wetstein in 1752, found also two letters of St. Clement in a manuscript copy of a *Syriac New Testament*.

These facts already amply demonstrate the Roman See as the axle, as the heart of the mystic body of Christ, which is His Church; as the centre and moving power of that communion of churches, congregations, and individuals, from which we received, first the unwritten, and then the written word of God.

No sooner had the apostles, and their fellow-labourers and immediate successors, established the faith, wherever there was a posibility of carrying it, than occasions arose, as has been shown in this work, to commit to writing several short histories of our blessed Saviour's life, to address several letters, independent of each other, to various congregations and individuals, as also letters to the Church at large. These letters, being addressed to all the faithful, and on that account also, like the Church herself, called

Catholic, were no doubt speedily multiplied by copies and translations, to be carried to the different churches that had been founded. The other portions of the Scriptures, written for special purposes, for special churches, congregations, and individuals, were, it is reasonable to suppose, less eagerly diffused, there being, as it were, no necessity for it, as they had not been intended, still less than the Catholic epistles, as rules of faith, but only to meet certain exigencies. Even the Catholic epistles may not have been propagated with any particular dispatch, might not even have been hurried all over the Church if there had been linen-paper, steam presses, and copying machines, in as much as there is no command, not even a recommendation, to be found anywhere, to supply the Churches with their contents: a sure sign of their never having, though Catholic or Universal, been intended or held as a rule of faith. The only instance of a request, to have the contents of apostolic letters communicated, not to other churches, but to one Church only, we find in the epistle of St. Paul to the Colossians, in which he tells them, to have it read to the Laodiceans, and to have an epistle, which he had evidently addressed to these, read amongst them.

Wishing the Colossians, to communicate the epistle he had sent them, to one Church only, at once proclaims its not having been intended as a rule of faith for the rest, even if it had been one for them. On the other hand, if the writings of the apostles and their successors, like St. Mark and St. Luke, had singly or collectively been intended as a rule of faith, that rule would be deficient, owing to the loss of this epistle of St. Paul to the Laodiceans, and no doubt through the loss of many a document written by the apostles, and of which we know nothing.

When however this exchange between the Colossians and the Laodiceans took place: with the *exact* copy, there was also conveyed the intelligence, that the respective epistles were written under the inspiration of the Holy Ghost; and this fact, coming from pastor to pastor, from bishop to bishop, these books became, upon undoubted and undubitable evidence, a canon of Scripture. Or, if the knowledge of being written under the inspiration of the Holy Ghost did not accompany either original or copy, it could not be established but upon the evidence of creditable witnesses to the fact, of witnesses who learned it from the author himself, and whose testimony nevertheless must have been unquestionable and conclusive before being received, as may well be imagined. For, here it was less blameable to disbelieve, than when Thomas doubted the resurrection of our Saviour.

That the Churches were slow in receiving this *absolutely necessary* testimony without which *not even the primitive Churches*, much less modern Protestant fathers, could decide, which was Scripture and which was not, is most incontestably proved by the fact, of several parts of the sacred writings being doubted by many for a very long period, not only as inspired, but moreover as genuine. When however through that constant communion of churches, that distinctive mark at once of the unity and universality, or Catholicity of the Church of Christ, the concurring testimony of her pastors *as to a fact*, not *as to an opinion*, became preponderating, overwhelming: then that, which hitherto had been doubtful, became to the doubting branch or portion, a sacred rule or canon. Thus by degrees, through that ever active, never ending "communion of the saints" on earth, the canon of the Scriptures, as the Catholic Bible contains them, was established; book after book was admitted from one church into another, as would be the children and childrens' children of a widely spread family, assembled in grand family council, where none but legitimate offspring are received.

Now, if any man of ordinary intellect, would, without hesitation, receive the solemn declaration *of a fact,* of such and such a book or books being canonical or legitimate, from such an assembly of the pastors of the Church, considered but as mortals merely: what credence would he not bestow upon the declaration of the selfsame assembly, if he knew that in their decisions they were moreover guided by the Holy Ghost? For, in the first instance, Christ said to the pastors, whom He himself ordained, "I am with you to the end of the world," (St. Mark xxvii. 20); "the Paraclete, *the spirit of truth*, shall abide with you for ever," (St. John xiv. 16, 17); and St. Paul says further, that "the Church is the pillar and ground of truth," (1 Tim. iii. 15), against whom, our Saviour promised "the gates of hell should not prevail." (St. Matth. xvi. 18): by which promises, the decisions of the Church, the declared and concurrent testimony of her pastors, become an infallible truth. For, even without the promise of the Holy Ghost, but simply with that, of the gates of hell never to be allowed to prevail against her, the decrees in matters of faith of these assembled pastors would have been still infallible, in as much as hell would have prevailed, falsified the prediction and promises of Christ, if the decision had been wrong and led the faithful into error. As God, as Christ, is without a particle of error, so must be His Church, which is both the body of Christ and His spouse; from that moment, in which her decrees in *matters of faith* partook of the smallest error, she would have ceased to be the Church of Christ. For this reason, no church, no sect, can claim to be of Christ, in which errors and calumnies are propagated, whether by preaching, or by the diffusion of corrupted bibles, and denying the canonicity of part of the scriptures.

What, in the name of common intellect, could or can be the value of opinions, doubts or denials, of any of the canonical writings, on the part of single or several individuals, severed from the communion of all these churches; severed from the tradition, from the concurrent testimony of the pastors of the Church, when even the opinions, doubts, or denials of individual fathers, eminent though in learning and virtue, and of individual churches, weighed but as a feather against the evidence of the whole. And here again you must particularly observe, and keep in mind the distinction, that the aggregate pastors of the churches of every nation in council assembled, declared nothing but *facts*, against which individuals advanced but *opinions*. And if in primitive times the agreement in all *matters of faith* of but a few countries, of a small circle as it were, was the only and truest test of their truth, how irresistible must and ought not to be this test, when we see from generation to generation, from age to age, from country to country, the continuation of this wonderful and miraculous agreement, until it embraces the whole earth, hundreds of millions of people, and presenting itself again to mankind at the extraordinary Council of Trent, convoked to combat the individual *opinions*, the cherished palliatives of an easy and luxurious life, of a few men, like Luther, Calvin, and some others, themselves disagreeing amongst each other. But nevertheless, and notwithstanding the far more striking contrast between these men and the Church of the world, than that between the heretics and the Church in primitive times, they were followed by multitudes of wicked, lax, indifferent or unreasoning people.

At that great council, that vast assembly of the pastors of the Church, still attended by the promises of Christ, and guided by the Holy Ghost, the Spirit of Truth; still as secure against the gates of hell as in the early ages: no new *facts* respecting the canon of the Scriptures, such as it is in Catholic Bibles, and such as it also exists in the Greek schismatic church, were then declared; but ónly a previous decision respecting this canon was confirmed, namely, that of the third Council of Carthage, held in the year 397.—In this Council, by the concurring testimony of all the fathers, the canon of the Scriptures was finally fixed. It contains:

OF THE OLD TESTAMENT,

Five books of Moses; that is, Genesis, Exodus, Leviticus, Numbers, Deuteronomy.
Joshue, Judges, Ruth.
Four of the Kings.
Two of Paralipomenon.
The first and second of Esdras, which is called Nehemias.
Tobias, Judith, Easter, Job, David's Psalter of 150 Psalms, Proverbs, Ecclesiastes, Canticles, Wisdom, Ecclesiasticus, Isaias, Jeremias, with Baruch, Ezechiel, Daniel.
Twelve lesser prophets; that is, Osee, Joel, Amos, Abdias, Jonas, Micheas, Nahum, Habacuc, Sophonias, Aggeus, Zacharias, Malachias.
The first and second of the Maccabees.

OF THE NEW TESTAMENT,

All those reviewed at the commencement of this work.

Now upon what evidence, what else than mere *opinion, caprice,* or *evil intent*, could a few individuals, so-called Reformers, not agreeing amongst themselves in anything, except in hatred of the Catholic Church, reject any of these books as uncanonical, against the universal acknowledgement of the whole of the then Christian churches, the Catholic and the Greek, and all the Eastern Christian denominations for from 1100 to 1500 years? What *opinions, conjectures* and *assertions* can for a moment, for the twinkling of an eye, weigh with any honest and candid mind against this stupendous fact? Nevertheless Protestants, unfortunately relying upon the partial, and very frequently dishonest representations and quotations of their own writers, without coming to us, to the old and uninterrupted fountain of all true religious knowledge, without ever thinking of examining *themselves* the witnesses of the unjustly accused party, reject, upon mere opinion, adopted from their teachers, several of the books of the Old Testament as apocryphal, simply because they are not in the canon of the Jews, and were not accepted for canonical, as they say, in the primitive Church.

These rejected books comprise:

Tobias, Judith, the rest of Esther, Wisdom, Ecclesiasticus, with the Epistle of Jeremias; the Song of the Three Children; the Idol, Bell, and the Dragon; the Story of Susannah; Maccabees I. and II.; and they fall under the decree of the so-called Reformers of the Church of England, which says, that "such are to be understood canonical books of the Old and New Testament, of whose authority there was never any doubt in the Church," but upon which decree almost none of the books of the New Testament ought to be admitted by her, almost all, or part of them, as in primitive times was quite natural, having formerly been doubted of, according to what we have seen under their respective hands. Why does she above all, admit the Epistle of St. James, of which Luther, the father of the so-called Reformation, not only wrote in his Captivity of Babylon (t. xi. 86): "that this epistle seems not to be St. James', nor worthy of the apostolic spirit," but actually cut it off from the canon of the Scripture, as he did with whatever was not in accord with his opinions. Good works and the Sacrament of Extreme Unction (v. 14, 15), did not suit his notions, no more than they did Vitus Theodorus and the Magdeburgian Centurists. The former, a Protestant preacher at Nuremberg, writes thus: "The Epistle of James and Apocalypse of John, we have of set purpose left out, because the Epistle of James is not only in certain places reprovable, where he too much advances work against faith; but also his doctrine throughout is patched together with divers pieces, whereof no one agrees with another" (In Annot: in Nov. Test: pag. ult); and the Centurists say (Cent. i., 1, 2, c. 4, col. 54), that "the Epistle of James much swerves from the analogy of the apostolical doctrine, whereas it ascribes justification not only to faith, but to works, and calls the law, a law of liberty."

Do you not, my dear reader, consider these dogmatical assertions, by men, in no manner whatsoever superior to yourself, except *perhaps* in a little knowledge of Hebrew, Greek, or Latin, the height of barefaced impudence? However, from what has been said, it will already be apparent to the honest reader, that the chief cause, which induced the nick-named Reformers to reject certain books, was no other, than that they were so manifestly against those heresies, which they sought each one his own, to propagate. This appears very plainly also from those words of Mr. Whitaker: "we pass not," he says, "for that Raphael mentioned in Tobit, neither acknowledge we these seven angels whereof he makes mention; all that differs much from canonical Scripture, which is reported of that Raphael, and savours of, I know not what superstition. Neither will I believe free will although the book of Ecclesiasticus confirms it an hundred times. (Whit. Contr. Camp. p. 17).

The denying of books to be canonical, because they were not received by the Jews, was also an old heretical shift, noted and refuted by St. Augustine, touching the book of Wisdom; which some in his time refused, because it refuted their errors; but must it pass for a sufficient reason among Christians to deny such books, because they are not in the canon of the Jews? After Malachias, the last of the Jewish prophets, there arose no other after him, to fix again the canon of the Old Testament, to add to it those writings, which from the year 409 downwards filled up the interval between that time and the coming of Christ; but He and the Apostles, as tradition assures us, acknowledged the Apocrypha as inspired Scripture, as is affirmed also of all these books by the Protestant Dr. Covel, who says: "if Ruffinus" (of whom we have spoken, p. 77) "be not deceived, they were approved of, as parts of the Old Testament, by the apostles." (Covel Contra. Burg. pp. 76, 77, 78.) Who then does not see, that on the acknowledgment of our blessed Saviour, the apostles, the tradition, or concurrent testimony of all the primitive Churches, proclaimed at the Council of Carthage, and confirmed by that of Trent in 1546, the canon of the Church of Christ is of more authority with all true Christians, than that of the Jews?

Respecting the care, with which the canon of the Scriptures was framed, if even the Catholic Church were not guided in her decisions by the Holy Ghost, let us hear Mr. Carpenter at page 227, where he says: "The circumstance of the primitive Church having rejected, for some period of time, three out of these five (Catholic) epistles, furnishes convincing proof of the great deliberation, with which writings, purporting to be apostolic, were received into the canon of Scripture; and also a sufficient answer to those who have charged the early Christians with want of care, and ourselves with credulity, in receiving as authentic and inspired, books of the original character of which nothing is known."

And this care, perhaps the direction of the Holy Ghost, will be more apparent still, when it is considered, that in her various councils the Church condemned, according to Calmet, 48 to 50 false and spurious gospels, of which he gives the list; that further she did not admit into her canon the Epistle of Barnabas, called an apostle, which he wrote to the Jewish converts; and that she did not receive into it the Epistles of St. Clement before spoken of, though they were attached to the sacred Scriptures, and like them, publicly read in the churches. W. Carpenter says: "It is notorious, too, that no book was permitted to be read in the primitive Church but what was deemed canonical; a proof, not only of the divine authority of the sacred writings, but of their integrity also. They were ever before the eye, and sounding in the ear."

You see here, my dear reader, how mistaken Carpenter is in what he here says, and what shallow grounds Protestants go upon; for, according to him, the Epistles of St. Clement ought either not to have been read in the Churches, or should have been included in the canon of the Scripture. However, the Church in both cases knew better, and who, but her authority could decide upon the inspired or uninspired character of these writings? Upon what other evidence than her's would you take the canon? Upon the opinion, conjecture, caprice, or evil design of Luther or Cranmer, or any other of their class; or upon the universal testimony, the concurrent evidence of the Catholic Church collected from every quarter? "Canon" says St. Augustine, "is an assured rule, and warrant of direction whereby the infirmity of our defect in knowledge is guided, and by which rule other books are known to be God's word: because *we have no other assurance* that the books of Moses, the four gospels, and other books, are the true word of God, but by the canon of the Church." This saint was present at the Council of Carthage; and who would not upon reflection cry out with him: "I would not believe the gospel, except the authority of the Catholic Church moved me thereto!"

In the same manner, then, in which the canon of the Scriptures was established, we shall find also, that to the Catholic Church alone is due, the

IV.—PRESERVATION OF THE PURITY AND CORRECTNESS OF THE TEXT OF THE SACRED WRITINGS.

It must be evident to the most unlearned reader, that the various churches, congregations, and individuals, for and to whom the gospels and epistles of the New Testament were written, would be very jealous, without even considering the imperative duty, of getting copies made, not only by persons, learned enough for such an important occupation, but also of that character and piety, so as to preclude any idea of voluntary alteration.

This precaution, this anxiety to have exact copies made, must have been greatest in those instances, in which they were intended for exchange between different churches, as for instance between that of the Colossians and the Laodiceans. For this reason, those copies must have been and were purest all over the Church, which were in the hands of the bishops and ecclesiastical superiors, of those "pastors and doctors, which Christ gave for the perfecting of the saints, and for the work of the ministry," (Ephes. iv. 11, 12, 13), and who for this purpose had them publicly read at the religious assemblies of the people, at divine service, the same as the sacred writings are to this day read in all Catholic Churches and places of worship. But apart from the interests of religion, for which clergy and laity were always ready to lay down their lives: it was natural for these copies to be kept purest,—though there may not have been many among the people, who in former times could read and write still less than now—as we find language itself preserved purest, the higher we go in the scale of society. That this was actually the case, we have seen already in the superiority of the Septuagint, which even the Jews for a time preferred to the Hebrew, and whose excellence we find mentioned above every other Greek copy. We find this fact

still more from the early translation of the Latin Old
and New Testament, called the Italic, and the preference given to it above all other Latin copies, until the
Vulgate of St. Jerome, for the same reason of greater
purity, supplied its place. And that the purity of
these works over all the rest was owing to their being
particularly cared for by the pastors of the Church,
is clearly evidenced by the fact of Pope Damasus'
instruction to St. Jerome. And though the persecutions, allowed but an interrupted and partial communion of churches, consequently but a piecemeal
collection and establishment of the canon of Scripture,
and rendering but partially visible the supremacy of
the Roman See: yet, there cannot be the slightest
doubt, that that very superiority of the Roman
Church, extolled by the Apostle St. Paul, originated
and decided also the character of the Italic, according
to the very name it bears, at once the indication of
its birth and home.

The existence of a translation, comprising the Old
and New Testament; of an Italic enjoying universal
esteem and preference over other translations, when
in Greek, mostly the original language of the sacred
writings, no such pure collection had been made: is
both the surest proof of an Italian authority, anxious
and capable of producing such a work; of an acknowledged and undoubted supremacy of the Roman
See, and of its own (the Italic's) intrinsic value. Had
the Church been less careful, had there been, above
all, no common centre to occupy itself authoritatively
with the preservation of the pure text of Scripture;
it is hardly necessary to observe, that there would
have been no end of diversities, no means of deciding,
which copies were true and which corrupted. Her
vigilance was not satisfied with having the correctness
of every copy, she used, rigidly examined; but, to
guard against errors in the first instance, she provided
rules and regulations for those inestimable men, who
devoted their whole lives, to what the Catholic

Church at all times considered a holy work, to the transcription of the written word of God. In the words of Merryweather in his Bibliomania, page 23, "in order to guard against errors with respect to the Scriptures, the most critical care *was enforced*. Monks advanced in age were alone allowed to transcribe them, and after their completion they were read—revised—and re-read again, and it is by that means so uniform a reading has been preserved, and although slight differences may here and there occur, there are no books which have traversed through the shadows of the *dark ages*, that preserve their original text so pure and uncorrupt as the copies of the Scriptures." At page 9, he says : " the pride and glory of a monastery was a well stored library, which was committed to the care of the Librarian, and with him rested all the responsibility of its preservation. He was particularly (page 15) to inspect and collate those books which, according to the *decrees of the Church*, it was unlawful to possess different from the authorised copies : these were the Bible, the gospels, missals, epistles, collects, graduales, antiphons, hymns, psalters, lessons, and the monastic rules—these were always to be alike in the *most minute point.*"

But the care of the Church went beyond the bounds of the convent, the school, or university. We learn from the same author, (page 33), " that by the University of Paris statutes were framed between the years 1275 and 1403, for licensing booksellers of *good character*, and learning, upon security, &c., and according to which they were not allowed to expose their transcripts for sale, without first submitting them to the inspection of certain officers, appointed by the University, and if an error was discovered, the copies were ordered to be burnt" (like Wickliffe's and Tyndal's corrupted versions of the Bible), " or a fine levied on them, proportionate to their inaccuracy. Thus the primitive accuracy of ancient writers was maintained, and they were transmitted to us through those ages in their *original purity.*"

By these means then, she prevented, detected, and banished the corruption of the sacred text, which, as it is in Catholic Bibles, was for 1500 years universally received by all the Churches, until a few individuals, unauthorised, called it in question; men, who, if properly viewed, were of far less weight, than those heretics, who in primitive ages, impugned the canon, as well as the text of Scripture. But neither the one, nor the other was to suffer in her hands, neither by illegitimate addition, nor by sacrilegious rejections and omissions, nor by erroneous and wilfully false translations, of which those, who separated from her, have at all times been guilty,* acknowledging their

---

* Having above, and in various parts of his work shown how it was *next to an impossibility* that errors could creep into the Scriptures by their passing through the hands of the monks: the author of "Bibliomania," either from an unconquerable prejudice against the facts, which he himself records, or from a wish, to lessen the contrast of Protestant corruptions of the word of God, he continues page 23:

"But as regards the Scriptures, we talk of the *carelessness* of the monks and the *interpolations of the scribes*, as if these were faults peculiar to the *monastic age* alone; alas! the history of Biblical transmission tells us differently, the gross perversions, omissions, and errors wrought in the holy text, proclaim how prevalent *these same faults* have been in the ages of *printed literature*, and which appears more palpable by being produced amidst deep scholars (?) and surrounded by all the critical acumen (!!) of a learned age. (!!) Five or six thousand of these gross blunders, or *these wilful mutilations*, protest the unpleasant fact, and show how much of human grossness it has acquired, and how besmeared with corruption those sacred pages" (alas! for the pure word of God in Protestant hands!) "have become in passing through the hands of man, and the ' revisings' of sectarian minds. I am tempted to illustrate this by an anecdote related by Sir Nicholas L'Estrange of

wickedness or ignorance by subsequent corrections, and of which some specimens have already been given. But besides these instances of the corruption of the sacred text, there are almost innumerable ones, which it would be impossible to notice here, and for which the reader is referred to the excellent work of "Ward's Errata," from which we have largely quoted, and from which also the following instances are taken :

In the early English translations, repeatedly mentioned, the so-called Reformers (!!) translated "temple" instead of "altar" in 1 Cor. ix. 13, where it says : "And they that serve the *altar*, participate with the *altar;*" they did this with the view of doing away with the sacrifice of the new law, for which alone an altar is required : the falsification was later corrected and the purity of the Catholic text proved. They translated in Ephes. v. vers. 5 : "or covetous person, which is *the service of Idols,*" into "*a worshipper of images,*" in order to do away with the lawful use of pictures and images. They did the same in 2 Cor. vi. 16 : "And what agreement hath the temple of God with *Idols;*" in 1 Epist. St. John v. 21 : "My little children, keep yourselves from *Idols;*" in 1 Cor. x. 7 : "Neither become you *Idolaters,* as certain of them ;" where in each case they substituted "images" for "idols," and in the latter quota-

---

Hunstanton, and preserved in a MS. in the Harleian collection.—"Dr. Usher, Bish. of Armagh, being to preach at Paules Crosse and passing hastily by one of the stationers, called for a Bible, and had a little one of the London edition given him out, but when he came to looke for his text, that very verse was omitted in the print : which gave the first occasion of complaint to the king of the insufferable negligence and insufficience of the London printers and presse, and bredde that great contest that followed, betwixt the univer : of Cambridge and London stationers, about printing of the Bibles."

tion "worshipper of images" instead of "worshipper of idols":—

All these instances of evidently wilful corruption, were later corrected by reformed Reformers of Reformers, and the purity of the Catholic text again exalted.

These are only a few examples, by which, notwithstanding the boasted translations from the Hebrew and Greek, the Catholic translation from the Latin Vulgate—not uncollated even in later times with Greek and Hebrew*—has been triumphantly vindicated, though properly considered, nothing is more natural. For it must not be forgotten, that the Latin Vulgate was likewise translated from the Greek and Hebrew, with this difference only, that then these languages were still living, whilst now they are dead; that then original and pure copies were to be had, whilst now the very reverse is the case; and still more, that the translators, by time and circumstances, by talent and learning, by morality and pious intent, were as superior to the falsely called Reformers, as the palace is to the hovel.

It would in truth be amusing, had not the consequences of the so-called Reformation been so direful to Christianity, to read in "Ward's Errata," how the continental founders of Protestantism, each one proclaiming himself a messenger of Christ, accuse one another, without exception, as falsificators of the word of God, fighting as it were, like robbers, about the treasure they called their own, and thus, by their very dissensions, and accusatory recriminations,

* St. Stephen, Abbot of Citeaux, alias Stephen Harding, an Englishman, monk of the Cistercian order, and who died in the year 1134, was a most learned man. In 1109, with the assistance of his fellow monks, he wrote a very correct copy of the Latin Bible, which he made for the use of the monks, having collated it with innumerable manuscripts, and consulted many learned Jews on the *Hebrew text*. This most valuable MS. copy of the Bible is preserved at Citeaux, in four volumes folio.

establishing the best evidence in favour of Catholic versions.

What with the many, many instances of acknowledged purity of the Catholic text, Protestants may still think of other corruptions, declared as such by the Catholic Church, it is difficult to say; an honest, candid mind, would for ever discard, even the best of Protestant versions, but above all, give up the foolish and dangerous notion, of taking any of them as his exclusive rule of faith. For, in the same way, that the Bible is resorted to by Protestants, for arguments, to confirm and support some previous favourite notions, which are fondly cherished as *the doctrines* of the Scriptures, instead of wishing to learn therefrom, with simplicity and without reserve, the whole will of God, contained in that one passage, "hear the Church:" the un-Catholic Bible was got up and translated by the so-called Reformers, not to learn therefrom the faith of Christ, but, as we have remarked already before, to elucidate the various religions which, without previous teaching, without previous authority, without inspiration, they all of a sudden, and of such a variety, adopted. Wm. Carpenter says so himself, in speaking of Cranmer's Bible, that, "after having received the royal" (and boyish) "favour of Edward VI. in 1550, it subsequently shared the fate of the religion it *was intended to elucidate*. A few examples of this object, this secret, in several persons perhaps unconscious, motive or inclination, to make the sacred writings conform to their previously conceived opinions and desires, will suffice.

To do away, for instance, with communion in one kind, with the real presence of our blessed Saviour under either the form of bread or wine, they translate (1. Cor. xi. 27): "Wherefore, whosoever shall eat this bread "and" drink this cup of the Lord unworthily," contrary to both Greek and Latin, which is "or" instead of "and;" contrary even to the translation of

Tyndal's Bible of 1534, and of Cranmer's of 1539, which have "or" like the Catholic text; and agreeing only with the Genevan Bible of 1557, as may be seen in Bagster's Hexapla.

To get rid of penitential works, they translate "repentance" for "penance," and "repent" instead of "do penance." With this substitution, however, no particular fault might be found, if Protestants were to give to "repentance" and "repent," that meaning, which the Greeks apply to these words, from whose language they profess to make this translation; or that signification, which our blessed Saviour gave to them, when (St. Matthew xi. 21) He said : " If in Tyre and Sidon had been wrought the miracles that have been done in you, *they had done penance* in sackcloth and ashes, long ere now," and in which verse Protestants substituted : "they would have repented," and Beza, "they would have amended their lives," for the Catholic text : "they had done penance." Now we know, that the Ninivites did penance, that they repented in sackcloth and ashes, man, young, and old, and even the cattle, *fasting* for three days. Imitate this repentance of the Ninivites, which our Saviour gives you as a pattern, and then in the name of God take which word you please. "Repentance" and "repent," express but the sorrow of the mind, it is passive, unaccompanied by any action ; but "penance," to "do penance," is that active sorrow for our transgressions, which shows itself in the performance of prayer, of fasting, of works of mercy and mortification ; it expresses that which our Saviour meant, and what the Latin Church, as well as the schismatic Greek, practice and carry out. That thus the fidelity of the Catholic translation is established, cannot be questioned.

One, to the Reformers themselves more individually interesting point was that of marriage, which in their own persons they patronized with all their energies, notwithstanding their voluntary and solemn promises to God Himself, to their divine Saviour, to lead a life of celibacy. Not to justify the breaking of their vows, of their own free will made to their Creator, not even as man to man might wish and try to varnish over, and to excuse, the breaking of a purely voluntary, not sinful promise; but to justify their taking wives, to make moreover the state of virginity, of continual purity and chastity, so highly extolled and recommended by St. Paul, an utter impossibility, and thus libelling the virtue of every man and woman, they translated St. Matth. (xix. 11), as follows:

Tyndal 1534. "All men *cannot* awaye with that sayinge."

Cranmer 1539. "All men *cannot* comprehend this saying."

Geneva 1557. "All men *receive* not this speech," which, corresponding to the Catholic version:

"Not all *take* this word," was again improved upon by the authorised version of 1611, by "All men *cannot receive* this saying."

In the epistle to the Philipp. (iv. 3,) they translate "yokefellow" instead of "companion;" but the best improvement, in conformity with Luther's well known ditti:

"He who loves not wine, woman, and song,
Will be a fool his whole life long:"

they made, and attempted to make, in the first epistle to the Cor. (ix. 5), which they translated as follows:

Tyndal 1534. "Have we not power to lead about a *sister to wife?*"

Cranmer 1539. The same.

Geneva 1557. "Have we not the power to lead about a wife *being a sister?*"

Authorised 1611. "Have we not the power to lead about *a sister a wife.*"

Luther 1534. "Have we not the power to lead about "*a sister for a wife,*" or "*as a wife?*" whereas the Catholic translation has it:

"Have we not the power to lead about *a woman, a sister?*"

Now this falsification must be evident to any one that ever read the Bible. St. Paul, speaking here of himself and Barnabas, evidently refers to nothing else than to an attendant person, a matron, to provide for their necessities: he could not write *wife*, in as much as he never was married, according to what he says 1 Cor. vii.; and in the words of Ward, "we have a little more reason to believe him, than those, who would gladly have him married on purpose, to cloak the sensuality of a few fallen priests." Asking for himself and Barnabas in the said verse: "Have we not the power to lead about a woman, a sister, as well as the rest of the apostles, and the brethren of the Lord, and Cephas?" St. Paul, in this reference to the other apostles, and Cephas, evidently speaks of an attendant matron, or matrons: he could not speak of wives; for, like him, they were also unmarried, or for the sake of Christ, and His Church, had left those, that were lawfully wedded to them; St. Paul, in fine, could not mean *wife* or *wives* with regard to any pastors of the Church; for if any of them were lawfully married, it would have been folly to excuse or vindicate or find fault with them, for carrying or leading about their wives, which rather they were in duty bound to do.

Luther carried his corruption of "wife" for "woman," still further than his English yokefellows, for which see the "Dublin Review," before mentioned.

As a conclusion to these instances of adulteration of the sacred Scriptures, the following must be quoted from Bagster's Hexapla, particularly noticed therein by the author. He places the six versions of the text, (Hebr. x. 23), thus side by side:—

Wickliffe, Tyndal, Cranmer, Geneva, Rheims, (Cath.), Authorized,
1380. 1534. 1539. 1557. 1582. 1611.

The first five have : "let us hold (keep) the confession of our HOPE undeclining," whilst the last version of 1611 has FAITH, instead of "hope;" upon which he says : " In this passage our authorized version has *faith* where the other five translations are *hope ;* the original" which is the Greek text heading the six versions of the Hexapla—"shows at once that *hope* is the right word. It is *quite inexplicable* how the word *faith* was introduced into this passage : it changes the whole meaning of the exhortation."

If it is inexplicable to Bagster, how this error could be introduced, it appears to us still more extraordinary, how the vigilance and anxiety of Protestant Kings and Queens, Ministers, Lords and Commons, Bishops and Parsons, to put the *pure* word of God into the hands of their spiritual children, should have allowed it to remain uncorrected these 239 years, when but a line, a word to the printer, would have removed the corruption.

Upon the original, as he calls the Greek text of Dr. Scholz, Bagster decides, that *hope* is right, and so no doubt it is. But who is Dr. Schloz, that his labours should be thus exalted into the touchstone of disputed Bibles, their texts and meanings ? Is he a pope, an arbitrator in these matters ? Does he set himself up as an infallible judge and guide ? Does he pretend, that his Greek Testament actually and for ever fixes the true text of Scripture ? Does he, set up his Bible for what Bagster takes it, as the standard of disputed editions and translations? None of all these, my good reader. Dr. Scholz, as we were gratified before to mention, is a Catholic priest, and the Church is glad of having such an exemplary and orthodox divine and scholar, as him, whose valuable labours are so justly acknowledged and prized by Protestant men of learning, such as Bagster. But they err, if they think, that their translations are more corresponding to the text, than those, which have the sanction of the Catholic Church ; and if to this venerable priest they go for the Greek, he will also be able to tell them the *true sense* of the same in their own tongue, and point out to them their errors. Will they trust him in *that* as well as in the Greek? If then Dr. Scholz, a worthy son and ornament of the Catholic Church, disclaims infallibility in his production: who are those others, by whom you measure your rule of faith? What weight, what authority, what position do *they* occupy in the scale of evidence, when compared to the testimony of the whole Catholic Church of all times and nations? Alas! for you, who pity Catholics for their credulity, in practically and truly believing in the "Holy Catholic Church," as they are taught by the Apostles' Creed. Or is it more sensible to believe, that Protestants, to whom St. Paul never wrote, understood and understand, for instance, his epistle to the beloved Romans, better than the Romans themselves understood it without any doubt or variation for 1500 years, before any Protestant Deformer was thought of? The very idea is preposterous.

Who, after all that has been said and shown, can still hold the Bible as a rule of faith without the blush of shame; and moreover risk upon it the salvation of his soul? Who is it that would not, for ordinary edification even, prefer the vindicated Catholic version, the version of that Church, which Luther after his fall, acknowledged to be true, and the faithful guardian of the Scriptures? For, in his treatise, (published about the year 1534, so many years after his revolt, and four years after the confession of Augsburg), for abolishing the private Mass, and in which he relates his famous conference with the prince of darkness (t. vii. p. 236), he concludes, notwithstanding his apostacy: "That the Church was the true Church, the pillar and ground of truth, and the most holy place. In this Church" he continues, "God miraculously preserves baptism, *the text of the gospels in all languages*, &c."

Who then again, as Luther even points out, cannot but see, that the Catholic Church is that rule of faith, which stands alone unerring among the erring, alone undivided among the divided, and whose genuine love for the word of God, whether by word or by epistle, has kept it pure and undefiled, has handed down to us the sacred volume in letters of purple and gold, and decorated with whatever human art could apply to it. Yes; those men, who spent their whole lives in the transcription and embellishment of the holy Scriptures, were not ignorant of what they wrote; they knew full well what important and divine truths and maxims they were adorning! These calumniated monks, unlike the Dutch printers and other propagators of corrupted bibles, for no filthy lucre, applied all their energies to these brilliant proofs of piety and learning; the glory of God and the salvation of their own souls, was their object. With these sentiments, and as monks, without any prospect, without expectation, without the possibility of personal worldly reward, without even the pardonable ambition of having their names handed down to posterity, can it be reasonably supposed, if even we had not the evidence of "Merryweather's Bibliomania," that they would pay more attention to the garb, than to the holy substance it enclosed? That they applied more talent and industry to the preservation of colours, than to the preservation of the purity of the text? That they bestowed more anxiety upon the shell than upon the kernel? No; their performances were not like those of the present day; theirs were no bibles all fair and beautiful without, and within full of corruption? No: the purity and correctness of the interior, was but faintly reflected in the beauty that clothed it, was likewise but a faint image of the assiduity, perseverance and success, with which the Catholic Church, assisted by the Holy Ghost, preserved the purity of the gospel of Christ and

V.—THE TRUE SENSE OF THE SACRED WRITINGS.

When the apostles went out to teach all nations, they every where founded Churches, to whom they left the entire deposit of faith, entrusting it to faithful men, fit to teach again. Thus, wherever an apostle had been, *holding firm even the form of sound words*, the selfsame doctrines were taught, whether delivered in the synagogue or in the market-place, before princes or in caverns. If there was any one, preaching to the faithful another doctrine, different from what they had learned, they did not receive him; he was not admitted into, or if within, excluded from their communion for novel teaching. For, St. Paul had told them, that if he himself even were to teach them differently from what he had taught them already, they should not hear him. In this manner, by this rule of faith, the Christian religion was propagated all over, and beyond the confines of the Roman empire, every where the same; those, who differed from this, every where the same, religion, were easily recognised, and, according to the advice of the apostles, shunned, avoided, excommunicated, as no longer belonging to the body of Christ, to the visible communion of the faithful. The body of Christian doctrine was full and entire in every Church, and could bear no novel addition; the concurrent testimony of the pastors, authorised and ordained by the apostles or their successors, decided what was doctrine constantly taught and delivered, in one word, they decided what was tradition, and what was new and hitherto unheard of; thus guarding the faithful from error and false teachers. This authorised teaching of every where the selfsame doctrines, was, notwithstanding every obstacle and persecution, in full operation, when the apostles and their successors had occasion to write, for, or to, their respective flocks, or to the various churches that had been established by one or the other of their number. As the famous

Protestant Lessing has it in his posthumous theological work: "The whole religion of Christ," he says, "was already in operation, before one of the evangelists or apostles wrote. The "Our Father" was said before it was to be read in St. Matthew; for Jesus Himself had taught His disciples to say it. The form of baptism was in use, before the same Matthew had written it down; for Christ himself had prescribed it to His apostles." And of this traditional teaching and the Holy Scripture, apart from the authority of the Catholic Church as the rule of faith, he says: "*that the Scripture with it* (tradition) *alone and without it is nothing.*"* Wherever then these writings arrived, the full code of Christian doctrine was already known, the traditional teaching *of the pastors* was the rule of the flock, and they read and explained the meaning of the gospel or epistle they received, to their people. As these writings were copied and exchanged, they necessarily were accompanied with the message of their authority, inspiration, purity of text and its meaning; if not, then these qualities could be ascertained only from the writer, or from those to whom he had originally written and communicated with; in fact, as we have seen before: by and through the testimony of the authorised pastors of the Church. And if in any uncertain or doubtful point, a lay member of the flock, had attempted, to give to bishop, priest, or people, the benefit of his advice and of his own interpretation, it would simply have been ridiculous; but if he had attempted, though high in station, to force his opinions and assertions upon the others, it would have been criminal, and the height of conceit and presumption. And yet, every modern Bible Christian, with astonishing tenacity, holds his own view of these points in question, for the only right one; and, where lawful authority alone should teach, and he should *hear* and *learn*, would fain wish, if by

* Lessings Theol. Nachlass, p. 125.

no other means, at least by dint of argument, to force his *opinions* also on others. With Catholics, the pope's, the bishop's, the priest's opinions, are only respected *as such*, and at no time would either fix the canon, correctness, or the sense of Scripture, unless supported by the subsequent testimony of other churches *as a fact*, constantly taught and delivered *from the beginning.*

Thus, with the gradual formation of the canon of Scriptures, the gradual transmission of their meaning took place, and was uninterruptedly confirmed by the concurring testimony, the traditional interpretation of the fathers, in proportion to their being able to communicate with each other. Owing to the stormy persecutions of more than three centuries, the transmission and exchange of the apostolic writings, must naturally have been slow; but, as for this very reason they were and could not be a rule of faith, it is palpably evident, that by an authority anterior and superior to the Scriptures, and as if they were not in existence, the full doctrine of Christianity, of the Catholic Church, was every where preached and developed; which would have been impossible, had its propagation been dependant on the written word of God.

Now, wherever any part of Scripture was received, its meaning could not be against what had been previously delivered; its accordance therewith was a sure proof of its genuine, as its non-accordance was as sure a proof of its spurious character, though the former of itself would be no proof of inspiration. In the same manner, that Catholics, but necessarily their pastors, would recognise that work as Catholic, which they would find agree with their doctrines believed and taught; in the same manner were the Sacred Writings *subject to the test of previous teaching*, to the concurring traditional interpretation of the Church, instead of their establishing, as Protestants maintain, the faith to be believed. The latter of itself, was an impossibility. For, whilst the Scriptures were in progress of collection; whilst very few Bibles were to be had, and still fewer persons could possess and read them; whilst, before the Catholic Church had authoritatively spoken, the learned men were doubtful of this book or the other, doubtful of this or the other meaning, doubtful whether Hebrew, Syriac, Greek or Latin was to be preferred; whilst confusion worse confounded, still reigns among non-Catholic Biblicists; whilst volumes were and still are written in favour of this and that, in condemnation of the one and the other; volumes too like "Horne's *Introduction*," which it bewilders an ordinary mortal even to look at, much less to examine, for finding out the safest Bible, text and meaning: what would have become of the saving and heavenly religion of Christ, what of the people to be saved? what divine, nay, what *human* wisdom would the man-God have displayed, if He had not founded a Church, unmindful of this chaos of confusion, unmindful of shoals and breakers, but firmly like a rock, though sharing in the contest and overriding all, to carry the selfsame tidings of salvation into every quarter, faithfully to deliver what had been delivered to her, holding fast in her powerful grasp the *form of sound words*, according to the injunction of St. Paul, and, securely and unshaken, taking her stand upon her divine tradition, whether by word or by epistle, upon the concurrent testimony of her pastors of every age, clime and nation.

Thus it was, amidst trials and tribulations, that she preserved also the true sense of the Scriptures as it had been delivered to her, as for 1500 years the whole world had believed, with the exception of "some who had separated themselves, sensual men, having not the spirit." The apostles delivered to the Church the doctrine of the glorious and real presence; the words of Scripture: "this is my body, this is my blood," could therefore mean nothing else; they

E

delivered to her the doctrine of the Sacrament of Penance, and the words: "whose sins ye shall forgive, they are forgiven, and whose sins ye retain, they are retained," could mean nothing else; they delivered to her the Sacrament of Extreme Unction, and the words of St. James (v. 14), "Is any man sick among you, &c.," could therefore mean nothing else; and wherever the Church found any thing not to agree with the doctrines, which the concurrent testimony of the Churches every where taught, she was sure that the writings were faulty. Thus, when Luther, in the text of Rom. iii. 27, foisted the word *alone:* "For we account a man to be justified by faith *alone* without the works of the law;" the Church and every practical Catholic was convinced, that an error or falsification had occurred, because this reading was against the doctrine hitherto delivered and believed. And if we are told by St. Paul, not even to believe an angel from heaven, in case he should preach anything besides what had been delivered, how could a *sincere* Catholic change his faith upon the reading of a book which he *knows* to have been falsely translated, and corrupted by some persons of modern times, because it is contrary to the previously delivered doctrine of the whole Church for more than 1500 years? If this were expected, and that Christians generally were to regulate their faith according to the various editions of Protestant Bibles and religions: though each reader were to take his own reading alone, without adopting the *opinion* of another, he would have to change his faith every day of his life; and if he were to be guided by the explanations of the multifarious, self-constituted dogmatical popes and teachers of these 1001 differently given texts, he would have to change it several times a day. Nay, upon one text even,* a serious Christian might

* On the clear parable of St. Luke xvi. of the unjust steward, Dr Thiess has counted already 85 different explanations among Protestants, and on the passage, Galatians

have to change his faith 50 times a day, and more, going merely by *his own* private judgment, and without being guided by the *opinion* (for, more than *opinion* they cannot offer), of others, if he were earnestly to consider, that upon the correct understanding of his own rule of faith, he has *staked his eternal salvation*. Is any Protestant reader *sure* for instance, *infallibly sure*, what the text means: "Unless a man be born again of water and the Holy Spirit, he shall not enter the kingdom of heaven." (St. John iii. 5.)? For, if he be not *infallibly sure* of its meaning, in order to appropriate to himself with *perfect certainty*, that, without which he cannot enter into the kingdom of heaven, what an *awful risk*, what a *fearful danger* does he not incur, in having but an *opinion*—reflect well on it my dear reader—in having but an *opinion* on this subject. No authority can give you the infallible meaning of this as of other texts, save that of the Catholic Church, upon the concurrent testimony of her pastors of all ages, and upon the promised guidance of the Holy Ghost. There are points and passages, upon which the Church has had no positive tradition, no positive concurrence of her ministers; and these she leaves to the free interpretation of her children, though she gives them her opinion, when Protestant teachers would impose perhaps upon you their opinions as matters of faith and fact.

What would have become of Christianity, of that *one faith and doctrine* left by our Saviour, if He had established no living and supreme authority, if He had left us nothing but the Bible, without an authoritative expounder and administrator? The so-called Reformation is not without examples to show you, what would have been the result. Look only at the

iii. 20, he has counted already more than 150.—See his work on the Impossible Union of the Spiritual and Temporal Power, page 17, note 14.

scene between the, *not by heaven* inspired, Reformers, whose quarrel respecting the Sacrament of the Eucharist alone, destroyed the common foundation of each party, each the Bible in hand. They believed they could terminate all disagreements by the Scriptures alone, and would have no other judge than that; they seemed not to consider, in the words of Dryden, that,

"As long as words a different sense will bear,
And each may be his own interpreter,
Our airy faith will no foundation find;
The word's a weathercock for ev'ry mind."

And so it proved; the whole world was witness, there was no end to their disputes on Scripture, even on one passage of it, than which none ought to be more clear, since it regarded a last will and testament. They exclaimed one to the other, "All is clear, and nothing more is necessary than to open your eyes." By this evidence of Scripture, Luther discovered that nothing was more impious and daring, than to deny the literal sense; and Zuinglius found nothing more gross and absurd than to follow it. Erasmus, whom both were desirous of gaining, said the same to them that all Catholics did:—You all appeal to the pure word of God, and believe yourselves its true interpreters. Agree, then, amongst yourselves, before you set laws to all mankind."[*] Whatever excuse they invented, they were quite ashamed that they could not agree, and in the bottom of their hearts, all thought the same that Calvin wrote to his friend Melanchthon:—"It is of great importance, that the least suspicion of the divisions, which are amongst us, pass not to future ages; for it is ridiculous beyond any thing that can be imagined, after *we have broken off from the whole world*, we should so little agree amongst ourselves ever since the beginning of the Reformation."[†]

[*] Lib. XVIII. 3, XIX. 3, 113, XXI., 59, p. 2102.
[†] Calv. Epist. ad Melan. p. 145.

With all this disagreement, the variety of interpretations and Protestant corruptions before him, Merryweather, at page 48 of his "Bibliomania," still considers individual interpretation of the Bible the *primary source* (!!), deeply lamenting, that Aelfric, its translator into English, as well as his fellow monks, "did not shake off a little their *absurd dependence on secondary sources* for Biblical instruction, still *sadly clinging to traditional interpretation.*" (!!!)

And now look again at the miraculous unity of Catholics, in virtue of the *original and primary source* of concurrent delivery, of firmly holding the *form of sound words*, and *sadly clinging to traditional interpretation*, which they foolishly prefer to the disuniting principle of personal private interpretation, which means, the principle of each one making his own religion, believing—not in Christ or the Catholic Church—but in his own individual opinion. Faithful to her divine mission, of uniting all nations into one fold, the Church could not allow this element of discord to enter her sacred precincts; she had received the office of teaching, the people had been commanded to learn from hearing, to obey and be subject to their prelates, to those who have the rule over them: and thus it was, that, when the African fathers condemned the infant heresy of Celestius and Pelagius, they—following the footsteps of St. Peter —laid for a foundation the prohibition of *interpreting* the Holy Scripture otherwise, than the Catholic Church, spread over the whole earth, had always interpreted and understood it. And so well did even Henry VIII., the respected father of the English Reformation, recognise and experience the danger of seducing men into the belief of private interpretation, that in 1540 he said in his preface to the "Exposition of the Christian faith:" "That, whereas there were some teachers, whose office it was to instruct the people; so the rest ought to be taught, and to those it was not necessary to read the Scriptures; and that, therefore, he had restrained it from a great many, esteeming it sufficient for such to hear the doctrine of the Scriptures taught by their preachers." Afterwards he allowed the *reading** of them that same year, upon condition "that his subjects should not presume to expound, or take arguments from Scripture."†

Though a brutal and apostate layman, the king had not failed to perceive, that nothing else causes those unhappy sectarian divisions among Christians, but the illusion of *private interpretation*, so expressly condemned by St. Peter, *that* modesty of every sectarian preacher, by which their model, Luther, was distinguished; for what this Deformer wrote in 1525, every private interpreter must in consistency proclaim of himself: "I will say it without vanity"—and yet what vanity and presumption!—"that for these thousand years the Scripture has never been so thoroughly purged, nor so well explained, nor better understood, than at this time it is by me." (!!)

If in Luther we are struck with his barefaced assumption of authority, declaring that he explains

---

* Henry VIII. as a complete Protestant, the first civil Pope of the National Parliamentary Establishment of England, was also the *first*, who since the commencement of Christianity *forbade* the *reading* of the Scriptures. For, there was no restriction whatever in the Catholic Church to that effect, until *after* the Council of Trent had closed in 1563, when, as the guardian and the pillar and ground of truth, solely owing to the flagrant abuse, which Protestants made of the sacred writings, she was compelled like the Provincial Council of Toulouse (see page 83), to *limit* —not to forbid—the reading of them to those, to whom in the opinion of the bishop or the parish priest, it would not prove unto destruction, but rather unto edification and increase of piety. This decree, not allowing the indiscriminate reading of the Scriptures to all her children, was a simple matter of discipline, not every where received, and has long ceased to be binding in any part of the Church.

† Burnet, lib. iii. p. 293.

the gospel better than any man living, in order to draw heedless crowds after him! we are still more astonished at the deceptive, and yet flagrant manner, in which the founders of the Established Church, likewise to blind the people, set forth a pretended authority. They, men, fallible like yourself, dear reader, but not so good and honourable, claimed this authority in one of the 39 articles, which is as follows: "The Church," which means a lay king, or lay queen, and the lay bishops whom they make,— "has power to decree rites or ceremonies, and *authority in controversies of faith:* And yet *it is not lawful* for the Church"—but what hinders her?—"to ordain anything that is contrary to God's word written, neither *may* it so expound one place of Scripture, that it be repugnant to another." But if she does? What hinders her? What *security* have you against it?—"Wherefore, although the Church be a witness and a keeper of holy writ, yet, as it *ought* not to decree any thing against the same, so besides the same *ought* it not to enforce any thing to be believed for necessity of salvation."

Here the civil Church Establishment claims authority, and yet *ought* not, by the last provision of one and the same article, to enforce anything to be believed! Can there be a greater absurdity? Can anything show more clearly than this, that she is conscious of having no divine mission, and therefore no lawful—though it may be legal—power at all: to "command and teach?" and how *can* she have it? For, in the words of Dryden:—

"How can she constrain her children to obey,
Who has herself cast off the lawful sway?"

But if she *have* authority, if she *were* divinely instituted, she *ought* to enforce it, it *ought* to be obeyed. The very expressions: "it is not lawful for the Church;" neither *may* it so expound;" "it *ought* not to decree;" "it *ought* not to enforce;" palpably proclaim, not only the liability, but the probability, perhaps the very fact of her doing the very reverse of what is *not lawful* for her, what she *may not* and *ought not* to do.

The true character of the Established Church was well understood by the Privy Council, her living voice, when in the late case of the Rev. Mr. Gorham they declared: that with regard to baptism, she taught neither one thing nor another; that she was so indulgent a mother as to allow her children to believe and practise whatever they pleased, provided they continued to pay well for such comfortable doctrine; for, if even she taught some positive truth, she was by her own article bound: "not to enforce anything to be believed for necessity of salvation," in order to drive no contributing worshipper from the Church, from the Golden Calf set up for the English nation. The ass of Balaam spoke, and so the Golden Calf has spoken; the established Archbishop of Canterbury, in his letter of 27th April, 1850, to the then Rev. Wm. Maskell, now, thank God, a Catholic, declares the same with equal candour, for there he tells him: "Now, whether the doctrines concerning which you inquire are contained in the word of God, and can be proved thereby, you have the same means of discovering as myself, and I have," as the highest dignity of the Anglican Church, "no special authority to declare."

In opposition to this, and contention with his superiors, to make *his discovery*, his view of baptism, the declared doctrine of the Established Church, the legal Bishop of Exeter, with an extraordinary valour, fights with the air, that is, with an imaginary authority in matters of faith, which does not exist, which his Church, to his own knowledge, in one and the same breath, claims and disclaims, and which therefore exists manifestly but for keeping some order in the approbation of what formerly belonged to the Catholic Church and the poor, though clothed in the externals of some of the garments and forms of the forsaken Mother of Rome.

But you, my dear reader of the Established Church, who, in 1850, have *the same means of first discovering* the doctrines of Christ, as your archbishops, bishops, and clergy have; how can you, (how can the land?) pay so dearly for, and in matters of faith, when your salvation is at stake, obey an authority, which for the purpose of teaching the saving doctrines of Christ does not exist, and which, if it exist in appearance, is *as fallible as yourself?* Is it not as derogatory to your good sense to submit to it, as it is preposterous and tyrannical to expect and exact obedience to its fallible teaching in whatever it be? The Church "has authority in controversies of faith, but *ought* not to decree anything against holy writ." But if she does? What is to prevent her, if it be not *infallibility* which she disclaims, and by the disclaimer of which she at once *abdicates* her *pretended authority*, and *absolves from all allegiance* the children seduced or forced from the Catholic Church. If the Established Church decrees any article of belief: who is to decide, whether it is against or conform with Scripture? Scripture cannot decide, for it cannot speak: who then is to decide between this self-constituted pretended authority, and those, who impugn her decrees and doctrines as against Scripture? Who is to be the umpire? By what standard will you judge the fallible leaders of your Church? By your own fallible reason? By some other fallible person or tribunal? Have your leaders, *who ever they be;* have you, my candid reader, any, and what authority, any, and what right, to interpret the Sacred Writings? Now if you but reflect, you will find, that neither Luther, nor your establishment or sect, in fine, that none of those who separated from the Catholic Church, under whatever name, pretext or motive, had or have not only no right to the interpretation of the Scripture, but not even a claim or title to the sacred writings themselves; they therefore cannot in fact justly appeal to them. For, they were carefully committed in trust by the apostles to their successors, to the pastors of the Catholic Church, and with them also their true sense and interpretation. Just like a treasure, entrusted to the safe-keeping and stewardship of a communion of men, of some institution or other; like the correspondence, like the documents of a family: those who separate themselves, have no longer any share therein, no more than perfect strangers. The Reformers, so-called, are like prodigal sons, who, forsaking their paternal house and home, and taking with them the father's will and testament, return again with copy forged, to dispute upon it the treasures they had quitted, and call in question the executorship of those, the parent had appointed.

And yet, these prodigal sons know full well, that the executors, the administrators of the Church were divinely and unconditionally appointed, subject to no human control or tribunal, because collectively not subject to betray their trust. The apostate priest is well aware, though his deluded followers may not be so, that these testamentary executors, and the children even, of whom they were the guardians, with loss of life and goods preserved the Scriptures, their purity of text and meaning; he knows how severe the penalties in early times, for parting with the material Bible even, and consequently, how *supreme* the authority of the Church, both to decree and to inflict them, and how anxiously she watched over this sacred pearl. And if this pearl could not be delivered without sin, into the hands of unbelievers, does it not show still more strongly than arguments can: that the sacred Scriptures were and are exclusively the property of the Catholic Church; and that it is more criminal on the part of Protestants, to appropriate to themselves, and corrupt the Bible, the unalienable document of the Catholic family, for whom they were written, and to whom they were addressed, than to burn this sacred treasure. The heathens destroyed the body, but Protestants kill the soul of the word of God.

Those Christians in the primitive Church, who for fear of torments and death, delivered the Holy Scriptures into the hands of the persecutors, that they might be burnt, were called traditors, or traitors, and guilty of crime, which bordered on apostacy. Upon repentance they had to go through a severe course of penance, and if in holy orders, they were to be deposed; but bishops had the power to grant a relaxation or indulgence. The Church still, on the second of January, commemorates many holy martyrs throughout the provinces of the Roman empire; who, when Dioclesian, in 303, commanded the Holy Scriptures, wherever found, to be burnt, choose rather to suffer torments and death, than to be accessory to their being destroyed by surrendering them into the hands of the professed enemies of their author.

When thus we see, in a manner different and awfully superior to the means of which we have spoken before, how intent the Church was upon the preservation of the shell: is it possible to suppose, that she should have been less anxious and severe in preserving the nut with all its flavour? No; she has proved it, as shown already, by the condemnation of false and spurious gospels, from the first ages down to the condemnation and burning of Tyndal's miserable translation, by the suppression of the Catholic Bruccioli's faulty publication, and by her standing anathema of all heretical versions, in which she neither did nor does condemn and destroy the word of God, but only its corruption and perversion by the powers of darkness, the work of ignorance and wickedness, though Protestants, alas! consider it their way to heaven!

From a corrupted Bible, no true faith, no true doctrine can be gathered; no more than men do gather figs from thistles; the correct sense and meaning is already lost by the corruption of the text itself; hence the anathema of the Church on such productions. To guard the faithful from the snares of Satan, she does not forbid the genuine Bible, which unto blood she cherished; but with St. Peter she condemns *private interpretation*, because from the moment of self-interpretation, *opinion* takes the place of *doctrine delivered*, the true sense is destroyed, it no longer accords with previous teaching.

The *necessity* of accordance with this previous teaching in all ages, for ascertaining and preserving the true text even, and meaning, if not apparent already from the concurrent preaching and teaching of the Catholic Church for four centuries before the fixing of the canon of Scripture by the Council of Carthage in 397, will appear as clear as crystal, when it is considered, that, according to Carpenter, page 47, "the sacred writings had originally, and for a long time, no punctuation, nor any such divisions as that of chapter and verse. The words were not so much as separated by intervals from one another. Letter was strung on to letter, and so continued, that every line was like a single word. Hence, the reader was obliged first to separate and recombine the letters, in order to form words and *discover the sense*. So late even in the fifth century, the New Testament had none of the ordinary marks of distinction, although Christendom had no lack of grammarians, who might have here found an undertaking worthy of their art. The following passage will give the uninformed reader some idea, though a *very inadequate one*, of the continuous form of the *original* text, and of the *misconceptions* to which it was liable:—

NOWWHENHEHADENDEDALLHISSAYING
SINTHEAUDIENCEOFTHEPEOPLEHEENTE
REDINTOCAPERNAUMANDACERTAINCE
NTURION'SSERVANTWHOWASDEARUNTO
HIMWASSICKANDREADYTODIE............

And what do you think, dear reader: was there any necessity, in the words of Merryweather, "sadly to cling to traditional interpretation?" Was there any previous teaching required in order to read, and to understand too? And was this previous teaching not the teaching of the Church? Was this teaching of the Church not also the traditional reading and interpretation of the sacred writings? Who could have read without being taught? But who could have understood, and correctly too, without a previous knowledge of faith and doctrine? And how could this faith and doctrine be derived and learned, except from a living, and in matters of faith, infallible authority? And again: who else could preserve this traditional reading and interpretation, except this very authority of the Catholic Church, in her Popes and Councils, the living and proclaiming voice of the concurrent testimony of her pastors? This is so clear, and the actual existence of an infallible authority, the necessity of holding firm the form of sound words, of traditional teaching, and the insufficiency of *any amount* of learning, (which again must be acquired from previous teaching), through which to arrive at the true knowledge of the Christian religion, of the genuineness, purity, and true meaning of the sacred writings, so evident, that it would be an insult to the reader, whether he be clever or dull, learned or unlearned, if an attempt were made here, to demonstrate this any further. As however it was no wish of Carpenter's, and not the object of his work, to sound the praises and exalt the authority of the Catholic Church and her traditional teaching, but rather to exalt the book above its maker, giving a specimen, in order to convey to the reader but a *very inadequate* idea of the continuous form of the original text, and of the *misconceptions* to which it was liable, our author continues:

"It was no easy task for a person *not long instructed*, or very much used to it, to *read* the Bible well and intelligibly, in the public assemblies, without adopting for his guide some marks of distinction; for private reading, also, assistance of a similar description was a disideratum. Hence arose the Masoretic punctuation* of the Hebrew text, and the Euthalian divisions in the Greek text. The date of the former is a matter of uncertainty; some refer it as far back as the days of Ezra, while others maintain that it was unknown before the second century of the Christian era. The divisions made by Euthalius, in the fifth century, were very different from those now made by the usual points, or grammatical stops, and consisted in setting just so many words in one line as were to be read uninterruptedly, so as clearly to disclose the sense of the author. Hugh has given a specimen of these stichometrical divisions, as they are called, out of a celebrated fragment of Paul's epistle, which Wetstein has marked H. The passage is Titus ii. 3. We give it in English, however, instead of Greek, for the sake of the unlearned:

* Masora means tradition, and is the title of a collection of critical remarks upon the verses, words, letters, and vowel points of the Hebrew text; the Jewish commentators engaged in this work, were called Masorites. Their system of punctuation, is a continual gloss on the law, and their vowel points, which served but to give the proper pronounciation and a peculiar kind of meaning to every word, were not known in any Hebrew writing in the time of St. Jerome. They were probably invented at the great school of Tiberias, about fifty years after his death, by the Jewish doctors, who fixed them as they had learned to *read the Bible by tradition*, in the same manner as our modern punctuation could only be made in the Bible *according to the sense in which tradition had universally delivered it*. The Masorites flourished from about the third century of the Christian era, though the Masora, the tradition itself, comes down from a remote period.

THAT THE AGED MEN BE SOBER
grave
temperate
sound in faith
in love
the aged women likewise
in behaviour as becometh holiness
not false accusers
not given to much wine
teachers of good things.

This mode of writing, occupying a large space, and as liable to misconception as before from the want of full stops, marks of interrogation, exclamation, &c., was by degrees improved, until offended grammarians, as Carpenter has it, began to introduce divisions and punctuations according to fixed rules; and this was gradually improved, but did not arrive at any thing like perfection, until *very long after the invention of printing.**

For reading the Old Testament in the Synagogues, it had been divided into parts, and at a very early period similar divisions were made in the New Testament for the service of the Church; for, the Scriptures, instead of being concealed by the Church, were from the earliest time, through all ages, the same as to day, publicly read in the Christian assemblies; and notwithstanding the continuous form of words and the want of punctuation, which made them

* In ancient MSS. no marks are found, except a point and a blank; before the 8th century it is very seldom one is met *with* any interpunctuation, and up to the 13th century, and later even, many are found without it. The comma is said to have been invented in the 8th century, but there were no fixed rules for the use of these marks, which were very arbitrarily applied until the end of the 15th century, when the learned Venetian printers Manucci augmented the signs of interpunctuation, and began to apply them on fixed principles; they were the first to use the colon and semicolon.

a difficult rule of faith, most likely better and more correctly read by the Public Readers of the Catholic Church, than they are now in Protestant churches and meeting houses, for a confirmation of which it is but necessary to learn what such readers had to pass through and to observe for filling their office. However, the books thus divided, were called *lectionaries,* and the sections themselves, *titles* and *chapters.* The author of these sections in the Gospels is supposed to have been Ammonius of Alexandria; those in the Acts of the Apostles, and in the Epistles were introduced by Euthalius mentioned before. The inventor of our present chapters was Cardinal Hugo, who flourished about 1240: he introduced them when projecting the alphabetical index of all the words and phrases in the Latin Vulgate. Towards the middle of the fifteenth century, Rabbi Nathan a learned Jew, undertook to provide for the Hebrew Scriptures a Concordance, similar to that which Cardinal Hugo had completed for the Latin Vulgate. But although he followed Hugo in his division of the text into chapters, he improved upon the Cardinal's sub-division, by numbering in the margin every *pasuk* or verse.

Noticing more minutely the divisions and notes of distinction occurring in the sacred writings, than has been done here, Carpenter continues:

"They form, as the reader has seen, no part of the original text, but are mere human contrivances, adopted for the purpose of facilitating references to the text, and of aiding our conception of its sense. That they are of great utility is undoubted; but it cannot be denied, that they are sometimes attended with serious inconvenience and evil."

"The punctuation is often very faulty. In some of the early printed editions the points seem to have been put in almost at random, and even in *the present Greek text,* as well as in *the English Version,* the *sense* and beauty of many passages are marred by injudicious and inaccurate punctuation. The misplacing of a comma will not unfrequently alter the sense of a passage; and the improper insertion of a full stop or a note of interrogation, must it is evident, be still more subversive of its real sense or meaning. Hence it is plain, that we should not blindly follow and adopt the decisions of those to whom we are indebted for the punctuation of the text: our own judgment and understanding," without minding the prohibition of St. Peter, "should be employed; and where a passage appears to be obscure or difficult, we may with propriety substitute such a mode of punctuation as will render it perspicuous and intelligible.* To do this with propriety, will of course, demand attention to the laws of criticism and interpretation."

What a wise rule of faith for mankind! particularly for the unlearned, or those who can neither possess a Bible, nor read it if they had one!

"The inconvenience attendant upon our divisions into chapters and verses is, that the *sense* is often interrupted, and sometimes destroyed, by the disjoining of what ought to be connected, and the connecting of what ought to be disjoined. The division of the chapters is frequently improper, but that of the verses

---

* The absurdity of this reasoning, the *impossibility* of correct punctuation, of fixing the pure text and meaning by any other means, than previous infallible teaching; and the danger of eternal damnation in not listening in matters of faith to that infallible teacher, the Catholic Church, will be strikingly evident to the reader, by referring to one of the strongest passages for the divinity of Christ, as it is pointed in the Latin Vulgate: Ex quibus est Christus, secundum carnem, qui est super omnia Deus benedictus in sæcula.—Rom. ix. 5. By substituting a point for a comma, Grotius and Socinus deprive the text of all its value: Ex quibus est Christus, secundum carnem. Qui est super omnia Deus benedictus in sæcula. "Of whom is Christ according to the flesh. Who is over all things, God blessed for ever. Amen."

is often much more so. There is in many places a full periodial distinction where there should not be so much as the smallest pause. Nominatives are separated from their verbs, adjectives from their substantives, and even letters and syllables are cruelly divorced from the words to which they naturally belong. By these means the chain of reasoning is broken, the sentences mangled, the eye misguided, the attention bewildered, and *the meaning lost.*"

"But independently of these evils, the divisions both of chapter and verse often exert an unfavourable influence on the attention, and induce, almost unconsciously to the reader, an idea of completion, or the contrary, very unfavourable to an accurate perception of the meaning of the sacred writings. It would be unwise," he continues in another part, "as well as unjust, to attempt to conceal from the novice the numerous difficulties which he will have to encounter in the interpretation of the Scriptures, and the large amount of labour he will be called upon to expend in his efforts to remove them. For a person to remain ignorant of these facts, is to be exposed to the constant danger of resting satisfied with the mere *dicta* of others, instead of applying at once to the source (!!) of scriptural knowledge, for the *discovery* of those truths, upon the immediate perception and personal appropriation of which depend his personal safety and happiness." He further, and with truth contends: "that it would be preposterous to take any commentators or expositors for infallible guides, in as much as they first form"—like *every person* from previous teaching—"an opinion of the sense of the Scripture, adopt a system of doctrine, and to support and defend it, the Bible is resorted to with the most inveterate prejudices and prepossessions, and every passage in Scripture must be made conformable, no matter what violence it requires. Being predetermined in favour of certain notions, before they read the pages of inspiration, passages of Scripture are strained, and tortured and darkened, by unnatural comments, because they are read, not to find out the sense, but to make them speak that sense which had been previously imposed upon them."

And this book is *the rule of faith*, which the wisdom (!!) of the world, and our author himself even, ascribe to our divine Saviour as having left to mankind, to the poor, whom particularly he came to save!!—

After this Protestant testimony, which might be much more extended, we are almost ashamed to recapitulate to the reader some of the evidence in favour of the Catholic Church, her canon, text, and interpretation of the Scriptures, and to dwell upon the credulity and want of judgment of Protestants, who risk their salvation on the Bible alone, when those so-called Reformers, who compiled or translated it, had in their teaching, compilations and translations no previous authority, no previous delivery to appeal to; had no concurrent testimony of pastors in any age to support them; no foundation for the Hebrew and Greek—even if they understood it well—upon which to establish their claim, even to be listened to. But, suppose that they had had the most perfect Greek and Hebrew originals of the apostles themselves; suppose that they had the most perfect knowledge of the Greek and Hebrew, even as St. Jerome, whilst these languages were still living: neverthless; their translations and explanations would still be condemned by the very authorities, from whom they would have got them. For, if a translation be true, and the sense properly understood, then it must agree with the traditional and universal teaching, with the *practical application* of the text and meaning by that nation, from whose language the work has been translated. And is it so with regard to the sense put upon the sacred writings? Do Protestants agree with the Greeks and Hebrews?—Most certainly not! For, the Greek schismatics, besides all other eastern

Christian sects, as well as the Catholic Church, cherish those passages of Scripture, by which *seven* Sacraments are established; by which marriage is neither a secret, nor a mystery, but one of these seven divine sources of grace; by which all of them believe in the real presence, and confidently invoke the intercession of the saints in heaven on their behalf; and as if to leave Protestants no excuse for wresting the Scriptures to their destruction, the Catholic, Greek, and eastern Christians, are joined by the Jews, to proclaim the consoling doctrine of purgatory.

No one will pretend, that Protestants, not even the enlightened and inspired Reformers, understand and understood Greek and Hebrew, better than did the Greeks and Jews, ever since the Old and New Testament existed. But to do justice to Protestantism: it also combines purgatory with the belief in the Bible as an exclusive rule of faith; for, if any person is to find out his *certain* and *secure* way to heaven, by finding out the canon, correct text and meaning of the Holy Scriptures, without the assistance of the Catholic Church: he will not only be in purgatory all his life time, but even then have failed to arrive at the gaol of his hopes.

Thanks, everlasting thanks to Thee, my dearest Saviour! that Thou hast given us Thy Holy Catholic Church, safely to guide the simple-minded through the doubts and vicissitudes of life! Thou didst institute this infallible authority, worthy of Thy divine wisdom! Those do not know Thee, who would have Thee to cast the sacred record among mankind, but to perplex, sow discord, and divide, where Thou wouldst have union, even as Thou and Thy apostles were united, and when Thy Church, visible as the mountain city, was to be Thy mystic body! Take away the blindness of those who say, that the written word superseded the authority of the apostles and their lawful successors, to whom Thou didst impart the Holy Ghost, and to whom Thou gavest Thy divine promise: "Behold, I am with you even unto the consummation of the world." However, long before this promise was made, God said to the serpent: "And I will put enmity between *thee* and the *woman*, between *thy seed* and *her seed*, *she* shall crush *thy head*, and *thou* shalt lye in wait for *her heel*.

Now there is a sense in the Catholic version, the parallel between the serpent and the woman is sustained, and the seed of the one and the seed of the other are left to the future to combat each other. But the Protestant version literally puts nonsense into the mouth of God by its rendering of the text as follows:

"And I will put enmity between *thee* and the *woman*, between *thy seed* and *her seed*, *it* shalt bruise *thy head* and *thou* shalt bruise *his heel*."

In the first place the parallel between the serpent and the woman, and seed and seed, is not kept up, which in *any* other case would be simply ridiculous. God did not say to the serpent: "I will put enmity between *thee* and the *seed of the woman*, but, between *thee* and the *woman*; yet the *seed* of the woman is to bruise the serpents head, and the serpent is to bruise the *seed* of the woman; and thus the *woman* and the *seed of the serpent* are passed over as if they had never been mentioned.

In the second place, the seed of the woman is made both neuter and masculine in one and the same act and sentence.

I think it would be next to blasphemy to presume that God would thus express Himself in a way in which no man in his senses, and knowing a little of grammar, would be guilty of; and every one will see, without having recourse to the original text, that this construction and rendering *must be false*.

By her immaculate purity and obedience to God's holy will, conceiving the "word that was made flesh," the woman *did* bruise or crush the serpent's head, whilst the serpent lay in wait of, yet *did not* bruise her heel; but the seed of the woman, in the real spiritual children of her own divine Son whom she conceived of the Holy Ghost, still lives; He still says: "Behold, I am with you even unto the consummation of the world." And the seed of the serpent also still lives in enmity to the seed of the woman; and that enmity likewise will last to the end of time, and is the key to all the heresies, schisms, strife, contentions, crimes, and misfortunes, in the world.

"He who is not for me is against me."

Do then, my dear reader, see carefully to what seed you belong, that *unconsciously* you may not belong to the seed of the serpent; Reflect!—reflect!—reflect!— before you proceed in your journey to death and to eternity, an alien to the Church of Christ. See by what an extraordinarily mysterious prompting—not of God—the Blessed Virgin and the seed of the serpent have been shoved out of the Protestant Scriptures, without even considering the many other corruptions made in the text of the sacred volume!! If, however, you be not convinced yet of the fallacy, of the Bible being the rule of faith, ask yourself still:

WHEN DID THE BIBLE SUPERSEDE THE AUTHORITY

OF THE CATHOLIC CHURCH?

which, as you see, unquestionably existed before this sacred book was formed.

Did the gospel of St. John supersede the authority of the pastors, whom he had ordained?

Did any of the epistles supersede the authority of the pastors of those, to whom they were addressed?

Did the Holy Scriptures supersede the authority of the Church, when they were circulating under the name of the "Italic?"

When did they supersede the pastors, ordained by

Sts. Fugatius and Damian, who, at the request of King Lucius, 182, were sent into Britian by Pope Eleutherius?

Was it when Origen compiled his Hexapla, that the Scriptures were exalted above the Church?

Did the Bible supersede the sacerdotal authority of St. Jerome, after he had revised, and newly translated it?

Did the Scriptures supersede the authority of the Council of Carthage, that stamped the seal of the Church upon them?

Did they supersede the Church in 431, when Pope Celestine sent St. Palladius to preach the gospel to the Scots? When the same Pope sent St. Patrick for the conversion of Ireland? When he sent Sts. Lupus and Germanus into England? Or was it, when Pope Gregory the Great sent St. Augustine to this country?

Was it, when at various times the authority of the Church condemned false and corrupted Scripture?

Was it, when Great Britian, under the spiritual jurisdiction of the Holy See of Rome, was called the Island of Saints?

Was it, when Wickliffe made a bad translation from the Latin Vulgate?

Was it, when punctuation was introduced into the Scriptures by Catholic hands?

Was it, when the children of the Church invented printing, and when, with her sanction and encouragement, Bibles were published in every language, edition after edition?

Or was it, when the wretched translation of Tyndal was condemned and burnt?

Was it, when Erasmus issued his Greek defective Bible? Or when Luther translated from a Hebrew copy? Or when he pretended like his co-deformers, to understand the Epistle of St. Paul to the Romans, better than they had understood it, always the same, for 1500 years?

Was it, when before the sixteenth century a few bad popes, out of two hundred and sixty, disgraced the chair of St. Peter by personal vices, for which they were personally responsible to their God? Or was it, when the tyrant Henry, or the abandoned Queen Elizabeth assumed and exercised the Papal authority in this country?

Was it, when at the Reformation the principle of anarchy was proclaimed in some portion of the kingdom of Christ on earth, in some part of the Church of God, each Christian taking the law in his own hands?

Or: when did the letter of credential supersede the ambassador who delivered it?

When did the compass supersede the pilot or the captain?

When?—when?—when?—echo answers—when?

And if, my dear reader, some person were bold enough to answer, when; there would still come the question: On what grounds? By what authority?

RECAPITULATION.

We now trust to have clearly shown:

That religion, to be true, must be divine, must come from the essence of truth, from God Himself; that therefore God is our rule of faith, and not our reason, because no true religion can come from reason, reason being itself a creature, a thing created.

That Christ *being God*, and for this reason of necessity, our rule of faith, instituted a Church, to whom He gave "some apostles, and some prophets, and other some evangelists, and other some pastors and doctors," but no Bibles, "for the perfecting of the saints;" who were to teach all nations the saving truths He had announced, and whom the nations were *to hear and to obey*.

That these dignitaries and pastors, having been appointed by Christ for the purpose just stated, became our rule of faith in His stead; for He said to them: "he that heareth you, heareth Me, and he that despiseth you, despiseth Me;" that therefore this rule, given by our Saviour Himself, *can only be reversed or abrogated by Him*, which no where, neither by miraculous nor other evidence, is recorded as having been done.

That some of these ambassadors of Christ, these messengers of the gospel, wrote certain histories of our Redeemer, and letters to different parties in the Church and to the faithful in general, for their instruction and edification.

That these writings were not intended for a rule of faith, much less as an exclusive one; that they neither did, nor could, in any imaginable manner, supersede the authority of the pastors, governing the flocks, to whom they were addressed; that in progress of time, they could not obtain an authority, much less in copies and translations, which they did not *originally* enjoy; that in fact they could never supersede the authority of that Church, from which they emanated, which alone preserved them, and to which they exclusively belong.

That only to the Catholic Church we owe the preservation of the Holy Scriptures, of which she was and is alone the lawful proprietor and natural guardian; and that from her alone we can infallibly learn, what is the canon of the Sacred Writings; that but on her testimony we are assured of the purity of their text, and the correctness of their interpretation.

That she scrupulously guarded the faithful from false and corrupted Scripture, never preventing, but always promoting, encouraging and facilitating the dissemination of *the pure word of God*, though from the time of St. Peter to the present day, condemning and anathematising private interpretation, which would exalt INDIVIDUAL OPINION, above the teaching of the very authority instituted by our Saviour Himself, above the concurrent testimony of the pastors of the Church of all ages.

That Protestant Bibles abound in errors and mistranslations, founded upon the *caprice and opinions* of the so-called Reformers; that without special and manifest inspiration, no amount of human intellect or learning, can ascertain, without the Catholic Church, the canon, correct text, and true meaning of the Scriptures.

That it would be blasphemy even to suppose, that the divine wisdom of our Saviour should have given us a code of laws, not only for ages gone, but inaccessible still to millions of the poor, *for whom He especially came*, and unable to read and to understand even if they possessed it; that it would be insane to maintain, that our blessed Redeemer gave this divine code, without establishing an authority to watch over, purely to preserve and administer its laws, when it would be a libel on the common sense of man, if we were to think for a moment, that he could make laws, without providing a magistrate or judge to dispense them, or that he could make a last will and testament, and appoint no executors.

That Protestants do not in *practice* prove the Bible their exclusive rule of faith, nor the private judgment of every individual as the highest authority; for, if they did, they would neither presume, by teaching, preaching and writing, to teach others the meaning of the Scriptures, nor would they continue to listen to others. Their acts condemn the rule they profess to hold, and they thereby show its natural erroneousness and inapplicability; upon their rule, *they neither have a right to teach, nor right to hear.*

That when, and on what grounds and authority the Bible superseded the teaching and authority of the Catholic Church, cannot be answered; and

That the Catholic Church alone is the true and infallible rule of faith.

CONCLUSION.

THE TRUE CHARACTER OF THE WRITTEN WORD OF GOD.

Yes, my dear reader, the holy Catholic Church is the true rule of faith, and the Holy Scriptures, are as it were, the sheet anchor of additional security; in her hands they are the compass, the mariner's chart, that never superseded the captain or the pilot; these, but not the crew, can moreover safely use them. But what would be the use of anchor, chart or compass, if previous teaching had not made them familiar with their nature and application; what would they avail the sailor, the untaught youth, if sent upon the boisterous ocean of the world without instruction, without an experienced hand to guide them? And what would even the captain or the pilot do, if anchor, chart, and compass perished?—they would be lost without the knowledge of the starry heavens, derived from those, that taught them, how to use the former.

So the Catholic Church. From her divine Master, from age to age, from pastor to pastor, did she learn and cherish the path to heaven, which constantly she taught and showed to man; her way lay through every country, but the path was every where the same: the glories of the heavens above, the storms and dangers of the world below. Nation after nation joined in her variegated procession, of which our Saviour led the van, followed by His apostles and their successors, and accompanied by all the faithful from age to age in uninterrupted succession, in one unbroken line; all the pastors wore the same livery of their Lord and Master, and their flocks received, all alike, the selfsame heavenly food, the rich and poor, the learned and the ignorant, the people of the east the west, of the north and of the south. When He, who led these multitudes into glory, was out of sight, many refused to comply with the strict conditions of the journey, dropped away from this united phalanx, perished, and are forgotten. Disobedient children charged their pastors with having changed the road, but its impossibility was evident, as no link was broken from the outset. However, more deserted, more fell off; in vain the pastors pointed to the unbroken chain, to the uninterrupted procession, to the unchanged livery, to the unchanged food; in vain did they show, that every thing accorded with the chart, with the compass left them by the apostles: they would not stay; the forbidden fruit by the way side allured them; they changed their name and livery, altered their chart, and so tried their unhallowed hands on the compass, that it no longer pointed to the one Church, to the one pole, but was blown about by every wind of doctrine, dispersing those that separated themselves, into every direction of sectarian quicksands.

Oh you! who see where the desertion took place, where a link was broken and the compass corrupted: return to that divinely guided procession, to that long, nay endless, fleet, headed by the bark of St. Peter, from which you were seduced or forced by *sensual men, having not the spirit to remain, that went out from it,* to show, that, in the words of the apostle, *they did not belong to it.* Look! all is still as of old, nothing is changed. The same rugged, thorny, and troublesome path of penance and mortification, instead of the deadening fruit of knowledge, *falsely so called;* the same glorious heaven above, instead of paradise lost; the same cheering unity in its diversified ranks, against the divisions and dispersions of those that left them. The Bible compass, which the pilots, which the Church had never lost, which she prized as a divine relic; which she preserved with her life; which she could and would not give up to to the mercy of a rebellious crew; which she still cherishes as an additional means to win you back to her bosom, accords the same as ever with her uninterrupted course. She alone can and will teach you its proper use, and impart to you such knowledge of the true way of salvation, that even without this compass, firm and unmoved like herself, you would be saved from shipwreck, saved from being tossed to and fro by every wind of doctrine, remain in the unity of faith and spirit, and safely arrive in those happy regions, where so many millions, by her hand, have gone before you.

As the most perfect compass, without the previously acquired knowledge of navigation, will not save the unfortunate mariner, that does not possess it; so will a corrupted compass be surer still to cause his wreck, even in calmest weather, in the most easy self-sufficiency and dream of security.

Alas! then, for those, who on the compass alone, rely as their exclusive guide to a better land, and yet think themselves secure! Look at the hundreds of sects, all one and the same compass in hand; and do you not see them steer in every possible direction? How has not that procession, led on by the self-constituted Reformers, that portion torn off from the endless fleet, at first so seemingly compact, been scattered to the winds of heaven? How many sects have not perished in the deserts, in the waves, and their names even been forgotten? And why did they perish? Because they made the Bible not only their compass, but set it up also instead of the Pilot, whom they deserted; they likewise made it their beacon. For, was there not also a beacon in the Church of Christ? This one, the hand of our divine Saviour had firmly planted upon the Rock of St. Peter, even so, that the gates of hell should not prevail against, should not extinguish it; He kept it nourished with His heavenly fire through the line of ages, from pontiff to pontiff; its light never changed, never varied, whatever the weather, however high the waves, however violent the storm; from whatever quarter beheld, it was always the same.

But the Bible, the beacon of the so-called Reformers, of Protestantism, was raised—who would ever have thought it!—upon their own vessels; just as their children keep it in their pockets, and kindle it with private judgment in their houses. And yet, with all this light of private judgment thrown upon it, the map of the Bible,—without the guide of the Church—is inferior even to a map of London; for, whilst this at least, leads men of ordinary instruction into the same desired street, converges multitudes by degrees into one common procession, the nearer they approach the place of destination: the other leads the most learned, as well as the most simple, into the most opposite directions, and instead of uniting, separates them the farther they advance.

And why again? Because this map of the Bible was not intended by its authors for the purpose, for which it has been perverted; because it has been set up by man as a beacon, in opposition to that of Christ; because, torn away from the anchor of the Church, from the lifeboat of our Saviour, without a connecting link from previous ages, to keep them in the saving current, vessels and beacon were naturally left a sport to the waves, tossed to and fro by every wind of belief, and wheeled about by every current.

But if this picture should not please you, my dear reader;—then erect your beacon on some newly discovered shore, on the rock of private judgement, and behold the effect! Does it lead men to union, into one procession, into one fleet, like that, from which they broke? Does it lead them into the harbour of Christ, surrounded by rocks and shoals, by difficulties and mortifications, by breakers of the desires of man? Most certainly not! See on the contrary, how these enlightened Reformers, of their own *assumed* authority, for once united, hoist this *new beacon* upon the *equally new foundation;* but no sooner is it erected, than the bond of union is broken; dashed against the rock of *divine* authority, they part—to reunite no more.

Deceived by the impetuous blaze of this beacon, multitudes followed their self-constituted leaders, and with each succeeding batch, the same effect is to be seen, and ever increasing. For, unlike the never changing fire of the beacon of Christ, its light was varying with every breeze, its colour changed with every mist, with every eyeglass, with every telescope, with which it was observed; it dazzled, blinded, flickered, took every hue, according to the eye, with which the mind of the beholder looked at it, different of aspect and form to each mind's different perception: and thus it was natural, that its worshippers should steer—and fail—in all sorts of directions. Instead of safely passing through, they ran foul of the breakers of the Church; one party was shattered on the rock of infallibility, another was upset by the tree of the cross; one division struck against the bulwark of the saints, another was wrecked on the cliffs of purgatory, without getting in; in short, separation followed separation, dispersion upon dispersion. The beacon, which, according to the calculation of worldly reformers, was to have kept men together, was to have united them more closely than before, is still splitting society into fragment after fragment; but instead of acknowledging its dividing nature, and returning to the beacon of Christ, to the Sovereign Pontiff, the centre of unity, they continue to cling to this their cherished, though deceptive idol.

And in truth; this compass, this beacon, the Bible, is in reality the idol of Protestantism; for, if you go about in this country, you will see it adored in every direction; perhaps, because it is capable of changing its face and oracles, with every new crowd of worshippers. What a wonderful image, and yet how different from the idols of old! Behold Luther within it, within the Bible! in a moment, his features are impressed on its pages, and the followers prostrate; the Oracle speaks: "*Real presence!*" Now observe the strongly contrasting countenance of Calvin in the idol, pronouncing the, as strongly contrasting, doctrine? "*Scriptual presence, real absence!*"—Cranmer enters; the same idol, another change, another face, another crowd, another oracle: "two sacraments only!" The idol now turns into a Quaker; and to a new batch of *inspired* friends, the oracle pronounces: "No priesthood, *no sacraments!*—It now is transformed into the features of Wesley, and its voice proclaims: "The Divinity of Christ!"—Another sudden transformation, and the idol is turned into the face of a Unitarian, the oracle exclaiming:—"No Divinity of Christ!—Christ is but a man?" And so on, change follows change, as crowd follows crowd; the accommodating idol looks "Independent," it speaks like a "Methodist;" it appears like a "Dissenter," and looks like a "Moravian;" in fact, every worshipper sees his own image reflected and in the oracle hears but the pleasing voice of *his own reason!* And this, no doubt, is the real secret, the cause of this extraordinary adoration of an idol, of such a magical variety of faces, the diversity of deceptive religions.

Look! how different the worship of the Catholic Christian! Neither in the Church, nor in the Bible does he behold his own image, but that of Christ: in her voice he hears neither the echo of his own reason, nor sees in the pages of Scripture the phantom of his own opinions or imagination; he hears but the voice of his Saviour, always and every where the same, whether speaking from tradition or the Bible, both proclaiming alike the heavenly doctrines which He bequeathed to us. These saving doctrines are the good seed, which the Divine Husbandman, at Jerusalem, entrusted to the care of the chosen stewards, to His *faithful* ministers, that, unadulterated with chaff and cockle, or spurious grain, they might scatter it all over the earth, even unto the consummation of the whole world. Wherever sown on congenial soil, its multiplying fruit underwent no change, because, as the characteristic mark of its heavenly origin, it was always to remain the same; and wherever you travelled, from village to village, from city to city, from country to country, from clime to clime, from nation to nation: in whatever place you discover this seed, you at once were sure, that it came from the same Divine hand, that first cast it abroad; for, there was no other fruit like it; you were sure, that no other but *faithful* stewards had scattered and sown it. And when you came into some northern countries, where a different seed, a different flower, a different fruit met your eye; you were sure it belonged not to the genuine stock, which you had found universally scattered, and yet every where alike; however, you were surprised indeed to hear it said, that, though so unlike to what you had hitherto observed, it was not only also the seed of Christ, but even the exclusively pure one. You were surprised still more, when looking more closely about you, when penetrating further into the pretended vineyard of heaven, you found not only a marked difference from foreign countries, but a difference of grain from county to county from parish to parish, from field to field, when even each field bore a variety of the most dissimilar fruit; and yet, each proprietor professed his seed to be exactly the same as the original stock. You were perplexed, you were bewildered; you knew that our Blessed Redeemer had sown but one kind of seed, and here He was proclaimed the father of each! But, when further still you went into the corners and recesses of the country, your anxiety and amazement were at an end, when with pleasing surprise, here and there, in some lonely unfrequented parts, a few spots in lovely bloom, though beset with penal briars and thorns, gladdended your eyes; for, you perceived at a glance the kindred seed, of which you had seen luxuriant fields in every land under the sun; your heart rejoiced, and yet it was sad, at these scanty remains of early and better cultivation. And indeed, hundreds of miles apart, these uniform remnants of former times might be noticed, which, though separated perhaps for more than 300 years, were still all alike; they all bore that peculiar verdure of recognition, by which the seed infallibily could be pointed out in every place; you were convinced, that none but *faithful ministers* could have sown and preserved it, amidst trials and tribulations. But how came it to be so dispersed and isolated ? How is it, that there have been left such miserable, though withal such lovely remnants? Alas! there was a time, when but few of Christ's stewards were vigilant and faithful in the land! the labourers of the vineyard rebelled, killed and banished the faithful ones, and took possession of the empire. The soil was then no longer tilled with the manure of penance and good works, no longer watered with the heavenly tears of fervent prayers and repentance; the head of the *faithful* priest was put into the scale with the head of a wolf; the bones of animals were valued more than the bones of the saints, and ease was loved more than labour: hence the degenerated seed, hence its endless variety, nourished by the same diversity of novel and experimental tillage, in which the plant of Christ will not thrive, in which it will take no root. When thus each little plot of ground had brought forth a different grain, when one plant stood in the way of the other, when division and degeneration from the genuine original seed could hardly go farther: how delightful was it not then, to behold the lovely blooming spots of the long banished, long persecuted Catholic Religion, multiply again, fertilising and beautifying the land, in proportion as the former were decaying in the chilling shadow of darkened reason.

Yes; thank God! the good seed of the Divine Husbandman, our Saviour, is again thriving; *faithful* stewards are multiplying again in the vineyard of Christ, retilling the soil with the original manure, to rear and reap an abundant harvest.

Come then, dear reader, to labour in the field of the Church, to assist in her harvest, that you may partake of her bread; make her your rule of faith, that you may be safe in the One fold of the One Shepherd; that in her you may again be incorporated into the body of Christ, in that grand and magnificent procession, of which He is the infallible leader; which for 1800 years travels on, in uninterrupted succession, and which, embracing the good of every nation, will securely conduct you in company of this army of Saints, into the glories of heaven. Yea, do not, like Jerusalem, ignore and lose the time of thy visitation, the call into Christ's alone saving Church; do not resist His invitation, but join the endless fleet, of which He is the Lord and Master, and St. Peter and his successors are the appointed pilots, whose line was never broken; join it, whether the sun be shining, or clouds obscure the sky; whether she be sailing in triumph, or whether He seems to be sleeping during the trials and storms that beset her course; there is no danger, neither from the hurricanes raised by hell, nor from enemies within or without; for, Mary, the blessed Star of the sea, that never failing guide, is always shining; Mary our Gate of Heaven, that gate through which He entered into the world, is always in view; through this Star of Bethlehem there is no deviation from the track of her Son and God; and as through her, whom to St. John and us He appointed Mother, the wise men as well as the shepherds found admittance to her Infant, their Saviour, so shall we but through her, the Help of Christians, the Refuge of Sinners, the Tower of David, the Mother of God, arrive and be embodied in the fleet of Christ, and find admittance in the harbour of salvation, in the Bethlehem of eternal bliss.

> Hail! Queen of Heaven, the favoured of God,
> Whom all generations shall bless;
> Mother of Jesus, who shed all His blood,
> To save us from sin and from death;
> Mary! my mother! so sweet and so mild,
> Pray for the erring one, pray for thy child.

PRINTED BY J. MILLER, COCKBURN STREET, EDINBURGH.

www.ingramcontent.com/pod-product-compliance
Lightning Source LLC
Chambersburg PA
CBHW020256170426
43202CB00008B/393